the Seer's Explanation

LARRY GOTTLIEB

ISBN-10: 1480152919
ISBN-13: 9781480152915

For my son, Luke

"For me there is only the travelling on the paths that have a heart, on any path that may have a heart. There I travel, and the only worthwhile challenge for me is to traverse its full length. And there I travel—looking, looking, breathlessly."

—Don Juan Matus,
as told to Carlos Castaneda

"It's much easier to ride the horse in the direction he's going."

—Werner Erhard

CONTENTS

FORWARD

Something happened one day in 1974 that would forever change the way I look at life. And I find that once you go through that door, you can never go back.

Imagine that each of us is a newborn fish. In the few days since we were born, we've cautiously swum about some, but now Mom has gathered us together to teach us about our world. She points out rocks, and that some good things to eat might be found around them. She tells us about the sand, and that there are some creatures that look like sand but that might sting us. She lets us know about what's good to eat and what might want to eat us, and eventually we come to feel as if we have this fish thing wired.

What she doesn't tell us about, of course, is water, because she doesn't know about water. You know, it's that water-to-the-fish thing: the fish doesn't know about water because water is all it knows. But imagine that one day something happens to you that takes you out of your well-understood reality, and in this case it comes in the form of a feeling of something sharp and foreign in your mouth. You're jerked around and pulled upwards, and suddenly you cross some sort of boundary and you can't breathe. You've been caught, and fortunately for you you're in a catch-and-release area and you're gently put back where you belong. And now you know about the existence of water. You know about water by experiencing what we might call not-water, so that you can now distinguish water from everything else.

For human beings, the water in this metaphor doesn't represent a physical thing, but rather an abstract idea. It takes the form of an explanation, a conventional understanding we have about the world and about our place in the world. We never think about this explanation, and for the most part we're not even aware that we have one. It's all we know. And the totality of how we look at ourselves, at life, at the world, our entire belief system, is based on this understanding.

For us humans, the conventional explanation is rooted in one fundamental idea: that the world exists pretty much as we perceive it to be, whether or not we are around to perceive it. In this view, the world is a machine, a mechanical reality that acts and evolves according to well-established rules. And yet any student of physics who has encountered quantum mechanics, as I have, will likely come to see that this view is ultimately untenable.

In 1972 I came upon a completely different idea of the world and our relationship to it. At first, it was an interesting and oddly compelling notion to me. But over the intervening decades I have come to see my attempt to grasp this different idea as my *raison-d'être*, as my purpose for being here, and I have finally understood that I no longer have any choice except to follow this idea as far as I can. It's as if I hear a calling, and at some point I finally decided to follow that calling as best I can.

This book sets down in words the story I now tell about my journey through life. All people, naturally, have a story they tell about their lives, and while I've had some wonderful experiences and encountered some truly amazing people, I don't think the list of events that have taken place in my life is particularly remarkable. And yet because I now tell my story in terms of following a path to which I was called, and because of the manner in which this new and very compelling idea shaped my choices and decisions, I believe that it's worth setting down. To some degree this is an autobiography, and there are parts of it that will sound that way. It's also an adventure story, but in a very different sense than one might expect.

INTRODUCTION

In the pages to come you will find an invitation. It's an invitation to consider a strange and counter-intuitive possibility: that what we see when we open our eyes in the morning is actually not the world itself but is rather our shared description of the world. Instead of awakening to the world and merely using a description of the world to think about and talk to others about our world, as our culture's explanation would have it, we are instead reemerging from sleep to the description itself. And I have found that that idea compels a reexamination of who and what we are.

To really answer that question requires a series of powerful exercises in abstraction. I would suggest that very few of us ever consider this kind of "Who am I?" question in the abstract. In the normal course of events, we take for granted our existence as separate creatures. We use the words "human being" to identify what we are, but we take the meaning of that phrase as a given. For most of us, being human is one of those unexamined predicates—foundational ideas— on top of which we place all kinds of other assumptions and conclusions. I hope to show that examining those predicates will call into question everything we've ever believed about who we are.

My intention in recording this story is threefold. First, it's for my son, Luke, so that he will know what his dad has been up to all these attribute these quotes with page numbers that refer to my first-edition copies; subsequent printings, of course, may contain these passages on different pages.

In the case of Werner Erhard, very little of what he said is available in printed form, and much of what I attribute to him I quote from memory. I spent a lot of time participating in programs he designed and a very small amount of time with him personally. I will some-times just call him Werner, as that's what we used to do. Although I have extensive recordings of Esther Hicks's seminar sessions, I also quote her primarily from memory.

One more note, this time about the sequence in which I present my account of this inquiry. Some of it is linear, as in a chronological sequence, but as a whole it's much more like a helix (i.e., in the shape of a coiled spring). That is to say, I will come back around to certain topics several times, but each time I will build on what's gone before. It appears to me as if that's the way my life has progressed. I continually come back around to certain topics and certain threads, but each time from a somewhat (and sometimes radically) different perspective.

With that, I'm ready to get started. I will begin this account by stat-ing my proposition in its most general form: The world we think we live in isn't what it seems to be, and furthermore, we humans are not merely who or what we think we are. In this book I will attempt to explain what I mean in such a way that someone else can, in a con-ceptual sense, stand on my shoulders and perhaps catch a glimpse of his or her life from a different vantage point, one that I hope will shed new light on who they really are and what they've really always been up to.

CHAPTER 1:

COSMOLOGY AND OUR CREATION MYTH

To get started with the inquiry into what it really is to be a human being, consider the notion of cosmology. Cosmology is the "big picture." Physicists who call themselves cosmologists use the word to refer to the evolution of the physical universe as a whole. In subtle contrast, I'm using the word to suggest the story we tell ourselves about who we are, about the nature of the world in which we find ourselves, and about how we got to be here and why. When I use the word "cosmology," I'm talking about an explanation. We human beings have explanations for everything; that seems to be part of what it is to be human. And the explanation I'm considering in this work is the one about who we are and what that world out there is. Before I present the alternative explanation that is the subject of this work, I will first summarize the explanation all of us already use, the story we tell ourselves, the one into which we live our lives.

I suspect that every human society, including ours, has a creation myth. According to Wikipedia, a creation myth is "a symbolic narrative of how the world began and how people first came to inhabit it."[3] Though one contributor to that online article states that all cultures

---

[3] http://en.wikipedia.org/wiki/Creation_myth

have creation myths, the article appears to me to be heavily slanted in favor of the assumption that cultures more primitive than ours have creation myths, and we, on the other hand, have science. That assumption probably comes from the use of the word "myth," which suggests "an idealized conception" and "a traditional story about heroes or supernatural beings," according to the *Encarta Dictionary*. So the first proposition to explore is whether we have a creation myth, and if so, what it might be.

We are told that first a world somehow came into being. How the world might have come into being is told as a story. Religious people of one persuasion or another tell a story about how God created the world, but I will use a more secular story. The current version of this story is that there was a "big bang," in which some unspecified but unthinkably small and unimaginably energetic "thing" exploded, and what we see with our eyes, our instruments, and our minds' eyes is the result of physical processes that this ancient explosion ultimately set in motion.

What is common to these stories, whether religious or secular, is that there is a world, it existed before we were around to experience it, and it continues to exist independently of us and any other conceivable class of observers. In the secular story, that world has existed for a very long time. It continued to exist and to evolve; life appeared after eons of time, and eventually creatures evolved with the mental and sensory apparatus required to see, hear, feel, taste, and smell the world, to experience it, and with the cognitive abilities required to think about it, to plan, to analyze, and even to understand. Even if your particular cosmology has it that God created that world with us in it, your explanation still rests on the assumption that there's a world out there that we human beings are a part of and which we also experience.

MORE ABOUT THE PREVAILING COSMOLOGY

According to the prevailing cosmology, the universally accepted explanation, who or what we are is an enormously complex collection of atoms that form molecules that form cells that form tissues, etc. This progression of collections proceeds according to strict rules, rules which allow for variations and new forms. And somehow out of that enormous complexity arose awareness, thoughts, feelings, emotions, and all manner of strange and wonderful aspects to "being human." The nature of the world in which we find ourselves is, so the story tells us, an equally complicated combination of matter and energy that scientists tell us has been evolving for some fourteen billion years and has produced planets, stars, galaxies, and finally, life. As for why we're here, the explanations I've heard range from predictable and/or accidental manifestations of nature's laws, to "working out karma or the paying off of karmic debts," to "fulfilling God's purpose," or to, quite simply, a feeling that there may not be any answer to that question.

But I'm arguing for the consideration of another cosmology. And this other explanation, this other story we could tell ourselves, is a completely different story about who we are, why we are here and now, and even the meaning of "here" and "now." It is at this point that a typical rational person would ask, "But is it true?" We may notice here that when one argues for or against an explanation from a rational point of view, our most important criterion for evaluating that explanation is whether it is true. And I will argue that the word "true," while useful in describing a particular fact, event, or situation, takes on a completely different meaning when considering an explanation for the world we experience and our presence in it.

With that background, I return to the question, "What is it to be a human being?" In terms of the prevailing cosmology, the phrase "human being" refers to a template handed down by the process of evolution (or if you're so inclined, created in God's image). The differences among us, as specific examples of that template, are accounted for by appeals to "nature" and "nurture." I refer here to circumstances of birth, in which genetic, societal, and environmental factors give us different combinations of attributes and paths through life. We should, of course, also include the results of decisions we make about what we should have, or do, or become. Ultimately, according to the prevailing cosmology, we humans are transients here on a planet that happens to be revolving at just the right distance around an ordinary star so as to provide the right combination of heat and light to sustain the chemical processes necessary to life as we know it.

We may recall the pseudo-philosophical question, "If a tree falls in the forest, and there's no one around to hear, will it still make a sound?" An equivalent question germane to our topic is, "If all sentient creatures somehow disappeared, would there still be a planet, revolving through space and time around a star?" According to the prevailing cosmology, there is no need to ask that question, and most people would find it silly. The degree of certainty with which virtually everyone answers that question in the affirmative (i.e., of course there would be a planet if we all disappeared) renders invisible any assumptions on which that certitude might rest.

If you accept the prevailing cosmology, and for the moment at least you leave a supreme being out of it, it seems to me that human awareness or consciousness must somehow be a byproduct of natural forces and processes. Now if you accept *that* explanation for the appearance of consciousness in the universe, I think your stance begs a few very interesting questions. Is it just a happy accident, a product of a particularly fortunate (or even common on a cosmic scale) assembling of the elements of our physical world, that physics and chemistry should give rise to biology and consciousness? Could molecular biology possibly explain the richness of human experience, the depth of feelings, or the pull of abstract ideas? Could it possibly explain love? Does that explanation really satisfy anyone?

It turns out that there are many disciplines that have had something to say on the question of how consciousness came to be (or even what it is), and what its relationship to physics and chemistry might be. I have studied a number of these disciplines to some degree, without being an expert on any of them. I will outline and discuss here my experience of some of the disciplines I've examined, because I see those investigations as a road map leading me to the development of my understanding of the idea that is the subject of this work. At some level, I always knew I wanted to understand how the universe works. I have felt that desire as a calling for as long as I can remember.

What follows is a brief autobiography, which from my current perspective can be viewed as a partial list of the forms that desire to understand has taken. Again, I generally try to avoid the hubris of thinking that my autobiography is important or distinctive in any way. However, as the raw material of an investigation into what it is to be a human being, it's all I have.

CHAPTER 2

BEGINNINGS

I was born in Los Angeles in 1945, on the day before the official end of World War II, so I qualify as a war baby by the barest of margins. I am the only child of a couple of very talented and successful classical musicians. They met as teenagers at the Curtis Institute of Music in Philadelphia. Mom was born in 1914, and Dad was born in 1916. Mom was an internationally known violinist. Quoting from a book about her, published in 2006 by the USC Thornton School of Music, "Perhaps the most all-encompassing career of any woman violinist in the last few decades has been that of the American, Eudice Shapiro, who has won prominence not only as a virtuoso soloist, an exceptional chamber music player, teacher and intrepid champion of modern works – but was for more than 20 years the only woman concertmistress-soloist in the Hollywood film and recording industries to compete on an equal footing with the finest male players. Undoubtedly through these mediums, her recorded playing in solo passages has been heard by an audience far greater than any other woman violinist in history."—Henry Roth, *the Strad Magazine*[4]

Dad, Victor Gottlieb, was a gifted cellist, though throughout my childhood I saw him as content to enjoy his proficiency at his instrument

---

[4] Evan Calbi, *Eudice Shapiro: A Life in Music,* p. 1.

7

and to support Mom in her career. Both of my parents became mainstays of the movie-soundtrack industry, and they wound up playing on hundreds of those soundtracks in the 1940s and 1950s. I often heard Dad called Mr. Shapiro at Mom's concerts and other public appearances; later in life I inherited the mantle. He made several trips to Puerto Rico in the 1950s to play at the Casals Festival in San Juan. I have a photo of him as first cello in a little orchestra conducted by the great cellist Pablo Casals. I know he loved those trips. He also accompanied Mom on her tour of Europe and many smaller tours in the United States.

In the summer of 1957, Mom was invited to participate in the Aspen Music Festival in Colorado. Dad drove us there, stayed a few days, and then returned to Los Angeles and to his work in the movie studios. While Mom taught violin and prepared for the numerous concerts in which she performed, I got to know the mountains, lakes, and streams of that wonderful valley on the western slope of the Rocky Mountains. I spent thirteen or fourteen summers in Aspen, and with the friends I made there, almost exclusively children of other classical musicians, I had an almost idyllic childhood.

I was brought home from the hospital to a little apartment on Franklin Avenue in Hollywood. Soon my parents moved us to the San Fernando Valley, known simply as the Valley. I remember orange groves everywhere, and the sweet smell of orange blossoms still takes me back to memories of that time and place. I remember a drive out to the Valley's center to buy fresh-picked corn. The air was always clean and clear, and I don't remember any of the extreme weather events that seem to dominate local newscasts these days. I do have one 8mm movie of me as a four-year-old venturing outside after the one and only snowstorm of my childhood. I look bewildered, and on my hands are a pair of oven mitts; I guess I didn't own a pair of gloves yet.

I attended Carpenter Avenue Elementary School in Studio City. Of the friends I had there, I am in contact with only one, and he is as dear a friend as one could have. Pete Luboff is the son of the late Norman Luboff, the founder and conductor of the Norman Luboff Choir, a leading choral group from the 1950s, 1960s, and 1970s. Norman wrote musical scores for many television programs as well as recording more than seventy-five albums. Pete and his wife, Pat, are gifted songwriters living in Nashville; they also coach songwriters and teach the art of crafting a great song.

At Carpenter Avenue I was close friends with Joey Funicello, whose sister Annette was just beginning her career with the Mickey Mouse Club. We lost contact after school. Many of my friends have nurtured friendships that began early in life, and their address books are filled with names from the past; that's not the case with me. The friendships I have mentioned are for me early examples of divergent paths. One can add layers of meaning to "lost" friends, such as "it's a shame you haven't kept in touch," but seen from another perspective, people do pass in and out of our lives; some reappear after many years, some don't. At some point I got to wondering why that is, and later I will consider an explanation for this phenomenon that doesn't have those layers of meaning obscuring it.

Like most of us, it was during my years in elementary school that a significant part of my personality appeared and evolved. I am not a tall person, and I remember how the teachers frequently lined us up on the playground in descending order of height. I was almost always at the end of the line, and I'm sure that part of the manner in which I have interacted with other people throughout my life was shaped as a compensation mechanism for the feeling of inferiority I had looking up at all my classmates. Later on I became aware of very subtle distinctions that were made among school-mates between Jewish and Gentile kids. We of the former variety always ate lunch on picnic tables set up on the blacktop, while the latter folks sat on the grass under the trees. One day I gathered my courage and ventured to join them on the lawn, trying to appear as natural as I could. I remember feeling as if there were a force field I had to press through to do so. Those considerations were of course entirely self-generated, though I didn't know that then.

A very close friend in junior high and high school was Fred Kuttner. Fred and I shared a passion for learning, and both of us would go on to major in physics. In fact, we would both go off to MIT after high school, though I didn't see much of him once we got there. Fred went on to earn a doctorate in physics, and he spent most of his career as a physics lecturer at the University of California, Santa Cruz. The book he co-wrote with Bruce Rosenblum, *Quantum Enigma,* is as succinct an explanation of quantum physics as I've seen, and I will quote from it later.

AN INTRODUCTION TO PHYSICS

In high school I discovered that I was "turned on" by physics. In those classes, taught by a man named Mr. Corben whose enthusiasm sparked my interest, I first felt the beginnings of an intellectual passion. The topics were basic, mostly classical mechanics and electromagnetism, and the lab equipment was rudimentary, but it did spark my interest. I recall feeling excitement when I grasped some concept he was explaining.

Later, at MIT, I specifically remember writing a paper in which I expressed the idea, which was clear to me then, that we can never know what something is, but only what it does, or how it behaves. For example, we say that some object reflects light in a certain way, light that then enters our eyes and creates electrical signals that travel to our brains and create the experience of visible objects. As another example, the electrons in the object's atoms interact with those in our skin to provide, through the physics of electrostatics, the experience of touch, and so on. Those verbs "reflects" and "interact" indicate that the object in question acts a certain way when we encounter it. But of the more essential nature of these objects—what they "really" are—so I wrote, we are doomed to be ignorant. It seemed to me even then that we cannot know the essence, the actual nature of anything we observe as long as we are observing with the five senses with which we're all so familiar. This idea became central to my current thesis, as we shall see.

A FIRST LOOK AT PHILOSOPHY

Along my academic way I also studied traditional philosophy and its practitioners' attempts to explain what human beings can know, an inquiry that philosophers call epistemology. Many of us can remember the names—from Aristotle to Kant and way beyond. I remember bits of many of my college classes. I studied David Hume, who argued that "humans have knowledge only of things they directly experience."[5] I remember reading Bishop George Berkeley, who denied "the existence of material substance and instead contended that familiar objects…are only ideas in the minds of perceivers."[6] Some also considered his arguments to be "a precursor to the views of Mach and Einstein," in that he questioned Sir Isaac Newton's pronouncement of the existence of absolute space, time, and motion (more about that later). At the time I found their ideas to be interesting and baffling, almost in equal measure.

I studied physics throughout my undergraduate years and about a year and a half of graduate school. In my memory, the material was presented largely in its rigorous mathematical formulation, with only occasional conversations about the underlying abstractions and the underlying meaning, what is "actually" going on. Occasionally, I saw the math as elegant, and for a while I found that elegance appealing. I considered a career in physics, but the elegance of the math wasn't enough to ignite real lasting passion in me. Apparently there was enough "juice" there to hold my interest for the duration, but after that stint in grad school (enough for a master's degree), it petered out.

A FIRST LOOK AT POLITICS

It petered out in the context of what I found to be a much more stimulating intellectual environment: the Vietnam War and the intense opposition to it among my fellow students. My search for understanding became redirected for a time to the political and economic factors that—as I saw it then—caused the human suffering of which I was certainly keenly aware, though it must be said, without my ever really experiencing it personally. As opposition to the war and to the "power structure" that appeared to support it increased, so did the pushback on the part of those who were committed to the status quo and who perhaps felt threatened by our activities. As I will describe more fully a bit later, things got dramatic and a bit violent,

---

[5] http://en.wikipedia.org/wiki/David_Hume
[6] http://en.wikipedia.org/wiki/George_Berkeley

and I fled to the next chapter in my life, what might be called music in the mountains and, occasionally, beyond.

FINDING A HOME IN COLORADO

I moved fulltime to Aspen, Colorado, in the winter of 1969–1970, and I discovered there a community in which I felt at home in a way I never had before. The way I felt then was summarized for me a few years later, when John Denver wrote the lyric, "He was born in the summer of his twenty-seventh year, coming home to a place he'd never been before." I had been in a rock 'n roll band in college, hardly following in my parents' footsteps, but thoroughly enjoying it nonetheless. In Aspen, I discovered a rich music scene, through which many famous and/or talented musicians passed at one time or another. Playing music with other musicians and friends has produced some of the most magical and enjoyable moments of my life. For a number of years it was a nearly effortless existence—joining with many other musicians in a wide variety of combinations, learning to collaborate and to perform in front of audiences large and small, and eventually in front of television cameras.

I was aware, at least to some degree, of how many other people would have liked to be doing what I was doing. Believing as I did in the cultural assumptions with which I grew up, I sometimes wondered why I was so fortunate as to be able to make a modest living doing what I loved, especially without any of the formal training my parents staunchly believed was essential to considering oneself a professional. I believed in the scarcity of viable spots in the music business, and so having one seemed a very fortunate situation, to say the least. I was also aware that holding a master's degree in physics from a highly respected institution while supporting myself playing music in bars did occasionally arouse the ire and frustration of my mother, who tried mightily throughout our time in the world together to understand just what I was up to.

With my nights occupied by the music business, my days were free for my intellectual curiosities to surface. One day I came upon a book about, of all people, Harry Houdini. In reading about his amazing escapes, I found myself wondering if he was simply a talented, even inspired, gymnast, or whether there was some kind of magic involved. Somehow, the idea that magic might be involved didn't strike this scientifically trained mind as outrageous. Looking back, I believe I was hearing "whisperings," or feeling a pull, from a deeper source.

BECOMING A SEEKER

In 1973 I came upon an introduction to Eastern mysticism, in the form of a young boy from India named Prem Pal Singh Rawat, who was known to his followers as Guru Maharaj Ji.[7] I felt in his presence the possibility that there might well be forces at work in my life that went far beyond anything I could then explain. Much like the Beatles on their journeys with Maharishi Mahesh Yogi, but without the fame and the cameras, I travelled to several places in the United States, as well as one trip abroad, to see and be with him, even if just for a moment. In his presence I felt a peace and joyfulness that I had never before experienced. Maharaj Ji said that those feelings were always within, and that with the practice of the meditation he taught I could feel them whenever I wanted. I have experienced that peace and joy in meditation in increasing levels of proficiency ever since. But as usual I also wanted to understand. I couldn't yet find a way to integrate his teachings with what I already believed I knew, and so I felt I needed to keep searching.

For decades my favorite source of images and inspiration has been Carlos Castaneda and his books about the Yaqui Indian man of knowledge, don Juan Matus. I came to accept that don Juan actually acted and spoke as Castaneda reports he did; it's also possible, I suppose, that Castaneda made the whole thing up, as various debunkers have claimed. It really doesn't matter to me, because what I feel when I open myself to his accounts of the "sorcerers' explanation"—for why and how things are the way they are—inspires me and continues to draw me forward.

Castaneda's accounts of his experiences while in don Juan's presence are largely centered around his fears and his physical and emotional turmoil as he struggled to comprehend that sorcerers' explanation

---

[7] http://en.wikipedia.org/wiki/Prem_Rawat

through his encounters with "allies", with the outlandish sensory distortions to which he was subjected, and with all the other aspects of don Juan's teachings. To my knowledge he rarely spoke of the awe and excitement with which I read of his experiences with don Juan in what he called that "marvelous desert". I continue to read his books over and over, because I continue to feel the "whispering" when I do so.

In 1976 I was introduced by my dear friend, and gifted singer/songwriter and guitarist, Bobby Mason to the *est Training*, a four-day course originated by Werner Erhard in 1971. That course was designed to allow people to experience, in one culminating moment, the distinction between the mind and the self, and to make available the possibilities inherent in making that distinction. I experienced that moment as a profound transformation that will stay with me forever.

In Erhard's words (to the best of my recollection), the mind is "a linear array of multisensory records of successive moments of now." In my words, the mind is a nearly endless, hyperlinked spinner of explanatory stories, decisions, and strategies about how to cope with the inevitable struggles of childhood. I use the word "hyperlinked" to reflect the mind's tendency to be reminded of topics that are similar to the one being thought about, resulting in the so-called train of thought. It appears that the mind's job is to make records of everything that happens to us, to record the circumstances surrounding events that have significant positive and negative connotations, to make decisions about what circumstances to seek and to avoid, and to do all this to ensure our well-being.

By way of example, I can say that based on some long-forgotten events, it appears that one far-reaching decision I made way back when was, "If I can get people to feel sorry for me, they'll watch out for me and take care of me." I don't remember the act of making that decision, but I see it show up constantly in the stories I tell about why something should or shouldn't have happened to me, stories that are commonly thought of as whining or complaining. That forgotten decision is like a fossil record, in that finding the fossil prompts a conclusion that the life form that became fossilized existed at one time, even though no one has ever seen such a life form.

According to the material presented in Erhard's work, we map these stories and decisions from childhood onto the struggles of adulthood without, in most cases, ever considering whether they are valid in the context of our adult experience, or indeed whether they were ever valid. When I whine and complain nowadays, I hear the echo of my early-childhood decision. I can see right away that my complaints are actually a technique for obtaining the sympathy of other people. If my experience can be generalized, those strategies may not be particularly effective for us as adults, and they certainly can't make us happy.

Anyway, somewhere along the way these survival strategies seem to become strategies for the survival of the mind itself. In the guise of a personality, with which we were arguably not born, we adults act in the world without ever considering that our personalities were to a large degree developed for the purpose of coping with feelings of powerlessness. Powerlessness, after all, is the inevitable feeling of an infant who cannot take care of himself and relies on bigger people for his every need. The upshot of this process is that the awareness of the being one really is gets lost quite early in childhood. According to Erhard, by the age of seven, "it's all over." He went on to say that a human being will sacrifice anything, including happiness, love, health, and self-expression, to obey the dictates of these strategies, and to steadfastly consider them to be the right strategies. As don Juan put it, "the guardian turns into a guard."[8]

I spent years participating in Erhard's work, in seminars in a class-room environment as well as in field classes that included a ropes course and other intensely physical exercises. These exercises were designed to allow one to examine certain elements of one's personal-ity and to discover for oneself that as coping strategies they are unnec-essary and so can be discarded. On the ropes course, for example, one

---

[8] Carlos Castaneda, *Tales of Power*, page 122.

can examine fear and discover that, in the absence of lions and tigers in our daily experience, fear is actually one of those coping strategies that the mind has adapted for its own survival. That course led me to wonder if perhaps fear is only of the unknown, and once the situation is known, the fear eases and finally disappears. In my first and only experience of the (initially dreaded) zip-line, that was indeed the case. Standing on the edge of the precipice, my mind screamed, "No way!" My body tensed, but my trust in the people managing the course was such that I stepped off the edge, and my fear was immediately replaced by joy. That moment of transformation will also stay with me forever.

More recent in my experience is a woman named Esther Hicks. In seminars she conducts, she enters a unique kind of lucid meditative trance and speaks in a deeper, clearer, and more authoritative voice than that of her more "normal" persona. She calls this voice "Abraham." In that voice, she speaks about how we humans are not simply these flesh-and-blood bodies—with the supposed "miracle" of consciousness—but really physical extensions of the energy that creates worlds.

In terms of her explanation, a portion of who we really are comes forth into this time-space reality. We do this with great purpose and with full trust in our ability to sample life, to make distinctions between what we like and what we don't like, and to trust that the totality of who we are will create from those preferences possibilities for us that didn't exist before. Our real, total selves then call to us on a new, "higher" vibratory frequency, inviting us to experience these new possibilities as manifestations in our physical world.

In this section I have briefly described my understanding of the ideas and methods employed by some of the teachers whom I have encountered in my search for understanding. I think one of the challenges of being a seeker of deeper understanding is that spiritual teachers often use terminology that doesn't map clearly onto the vocabulary used by scientists. I have sometimes found that this leads to confusion and incomplete understanding. In addition, I have found that no single teacher has left me with what I consider to be the completely satisfying explanation I have always hoped to find. However, I have somehow synthesized all these ideas with some of my own and come to a framework that seems to hold up pretty well.

In the next chapter, I will return to my earlier statement that, when relying on information accessible to our five senses, we can never know about the essence of something we observe but only about how we interact with it. That will lead to a discussion of the basics of classical physics, the understanding of the physical world that stood at the end of the nineteenth century. Classical physics matches up quite well with our shared, common-sense understanding of the world around us. I think this discussion will prove useful in grasping why twentieth century physics represents such a radical transformation in our understanding of the world we think we live in, and why we might want to acquire a different understanding of who we really are in the light of this new physics.

CHAPTER 3

THOUGHTS ABOUT THE PHYSICAL WORLD

A VIBRATIONAL UNIVERSE?

Esther Hicks tells us we are each interpreters of vibration. Suppose we consider that proposition from a scientific perspective. What would that mean? At first I found it very hard to understand that word, vibration, in this context. When I hear the word I usually think of something that's rattling, or perhaps of a generally uncomfortable feeling while in a moving car or aircraft. So let's flesh that out a bit more, because the idea is central to this discussion. I'm typing these words on a laptop that is resting on a kitchen counter. What is the essential nature of that counter? What is it <u>really</u>? Most people would say that it consists of some physical material, granite in this case. And what is the granite made of? The answer would be molecules or crystals of one or more substances, which are made of atoms, which are made of protons, neutrons, and electrons. That's just first semester high school physics.

A physicist might go further and say that these so-called elementary particles are themselves made of smaller components called quarks, and perhaps other essential things as well. A bit later I'll touch briefly on string theory, which offers a different interpretation of what those essential particles really are. But what do I really see and feel when I look at or touch the kitchen counter? As I said before, I see light bouncing off the counter and entering my eyes, and I feel the effect of electrostatic forces in my fingertips. In other words, in the context of my understanding of myself as a physical body, the scope of the information with which I can make sense of the physical world is limited to what comes to me through my physical senses.

So my interaction with the surface on which my laptop sits is limited to phenomena my senses evolved to perceive. But what is it that makes those sensations into a kitchen counter? I believe you have to finally say that it is an *interpretation* of those sensations that "makes" it into a counter, and without that interpretation we would presumably still see and feel those sensations, but the counter would just be a volume of marbled, brownish stuff that hurts if I bang into it and that supports other stuff and keeps it from falling on the floor. There's a layer of interpretation that lies between me and the object I am observing, and when I want to use that object (e.g., to hold up my laptop), it is the interpretation with which I am interacting.

At this point I am reminded of the young child whose father is a television personality. The child sees his father on the television screen, and that image on the screen prompts the child to go around to the back of the set to find Daddy. Essentially, the TV is interpreting, or decoding, an electrical signal carried by a cable and rendering the resulting image on the screen; the signal consists of a vibration of what is called the electromagnetic field. The child, however, does not yet realize that the image on the screen is merely a rendering of electrical data, not the "real" thing. I suggest that we do the same thing with the electrical input to our senses. My brain creates a picture of the world by interpreting the sensory data delivered to it, and I take that picture, that description, as "reality."

For his part, don Juan Matus said that we never experience the world itself. Instead, when we think or talk about our experience, it is the description of the world of which we think and speak. Here is the passage: "Think of this. The world doesn't yield to us directly; the description of the world stands in between. So, properly speaking, we are always one step removed, and our experience of the world is always a recollection of the experience. We are perennially recollecting the instant that has just happened, just passed. We recollect, recollect, recollect."[9]

That's a very different idea of "reality" than we're accustomed to, wouldn't you say? If we were to accept that idea as a premise, then the entire physical world we seem to be experiencing (i.e., that we see, feel, taste, etcetera) would actually be a description produced by interpretation of sensory data. Furthermore, we interpret that data as indicating (i.e., we make the assumption, we believe) that there are objects "out there" that have a hand in producing that data. And we can interact with one another because we share, to a sufficient degree, that interpretation. In fact, it could be said that our language evolved for the express purpose of allowing us to participate in that interaction. That would explain why it's so hard to talk about whatever it is that might lie beyond or behind the description of the world: our language evolved to represent the description, not the world itself!

In terms of this idea then, we humans continuously interpret our description of the world as indicating that the world we're describing exists as we describe it. How might we have acquired that interpretation or description? Both don Juan and Werner Erhard said essentially that the description of the world was pounded into us by our parents, relatives, friends, and so on from the moment we were born. In that view, the newborn starts out with a complex mix of sights and sounds and other sensations without the interpretive mechanism, and he or she must then learn to perceive the world the rest of us perceive so that he or she can function in the world and interact with us.

In other words, the child must become a member of the culture into which he or she is born, and that process of acquiring membership

---

[9] Carlos Castaneda, *Tales of Power* p. 53.

is carried out by absorbing and learning to perceive the descriptions offered. It occurs to me in this context that perhaps there are people among us in whom that membership status is not fully realized, and those people have a much harder time dealing with the world we take for granted, whereupon the medical establishment gives them a diagnosis and attempts to treat the "condition" with therapy, often involving drugs.

BRIEFLY, STRING THEORY—
THE PHYSICIST'S "NEW" EXPLANATION

Recently, more than forty years after I earned my degrees, I heard a physicist named Brian Greene interviewed on NPR. He was speaking about his new book on physics, which happens to be a detailed yet nonmathematical analysis of the possible existence of parallel universes. I was immediately interested, both because I have always had a passion for physics and because I know, from leafing through my old physics books, that the mathematics necessary for a rigorous understanding of most advanced topics is now well beyond my reach.

Due to Greene's talent for making the concepts of physics accessible, I have become a major fan. I have read and reread all of his books, and I have thoroughly enjoyed my new comprehension of the material. But it was when I began to digest his description of string theory that I had that feeling you get when the hidden plot twists in a good mystery novel start to come together, and you smile because you've just grasped the big picture. According to string theory, all of the manifestations of nature, the particles and the forces, are due to vibrating strings.

There's that word, vibration, again. But this time, it appears in the rigorous context of contemporary (though still controversial) physics. As I understand Greene's explanation, these strings are not to be thought of as objects in space but rather as vibrations of the fabric of spacetime itself. Anyway, strings vibrate, and the modes in which they vibrate can be associated with each of the elements of the observable universe. Remember those protons, neutrons, and electrons, and maybe the quarks and all the rest? Well, string theory says that the matter particles, the force particles—in quantum physics, forces between particles are thought of as due to the exchange of force particles. Don't worry about understanding that… just take my word for it—and all the other fundamental constituents of the physical universe are produced in our experience and in our instruments as interpretations, as multisensory renderings, of these vibratory patterns. Even gravity, which Einstein and his successors struggled to include in a so-called unified theory, can be viewed as the exchange of force particles called gravitons, and sure enough the mathematics of string theory has a vibrational pattern that matches precisely the graviton's required characteristics.

COMMON SENSE AND PHYSICS – TAKE ONE

As I stated earlier, I do speak a fair amount about physics in this book. In fact, one could say that this book represents my attempt to reconcile physics and what our culture refers to as "spirituality." And there's a fair bit more physics to come before we're through. But this is a good place to state my purpose in its inclusion: I want to try to convince you, as I have been convinced, that what we call common sense, our shared "knowledge" of the world we live in, is not a good indication of how the world actually works. In fact, I hope to show that common sense, or conventional wisdom, actually gives us a picture of the world that is, in a strict sense, wildly inaccurate.

In case you think that's an odd statement to make, consider that in the arc of human history, it wasn't so long ago that people thought the world was flat. In fact, everybody knew that. And, if you were a seafaring man on the western coast of Europe prior to the 15th century, your travel options were rather limited as a result. You couldn't yet, for example, go to Queen Isabella in Castile and ask her for the funds to equip three ships for a westward voyage to the New World. She would have said, "Are you nuts? You'll fall off the edge!" Or something to that effect.

There are many examples from our history as a species in which what everyone knew to be true turned out to be just plain wrong. And we have resisted mightily that better understanding. Just ask Giordano Bruno, or Copernicus, about their experiences when espousing the idea that the earth isn't the center of the solar system.

But those guys were primitive compared to us. They didn't have the benefit of all the calculations and experimental results that have been done since. We are not under any of those powerful illusions like flat earth and geo-centrism. Right? But what if we really are like those fish I spoke about in the Forward to this book?

NOW, GENTLY, BACK TO PHYSICS

Let's return to this idea that the building blocks of "solid" reality are in actuality simply vibrations in the fabric called spacetime. As a way of picturing these vibrational patterns, think about a wind instrument, say a French horn. What gives that lovely instrument its distinctive sound? Someone who listens to classical music knows it immediately when they hear it. If the horn player plays a particular note, it doesn't sound like the same note played on any other instrument or any other device capable of producing that note. What makes the difference? In the case of such a wind instrument, the note is shaped or formed by the instrument's architecture, the specific dimensions of the brass pipes of which it is made, the location and radii of the turns the pipes make, and so on. If we could see the sound waves, the vibrations that those architectural characteristics produce in the air as the player blows through the horn, we would expect that those vibratory patterns would conform in some way to the contours of the horn itself.

When I read Brian Greene's wonderful description of some of the elements of string theory, I'm struck by the fact that mathematical physicists working on the details of the theory have apparently found that, in order to make the math consistent, ten spatial dimensions must be postulated. When I first heard that, I was temporarily convinced that physicists were heading off in some bizarre direction. How could space possibly consist of ten spatial dimensions, when we only are able to experience three? I thought about this for some time before I remembered that from the viewpoint of my understanding of sensory input, and the rationality that interprets it, I'm only able to perceive how the physical universe behaves, not what it really is. That stipulation applies to space itself (actually, in Einstein's formulation, spacetime), as well as the objects we believe exist in that spacetime. In other words, if string theory ultimately proves useful in explaining the physical world, we could then say that the world simply behaves or appears to us as if it has eleven spacetime dimensions (that is, ten of space, one of time).

Anyway, Greene then proceeds to consider the question, "If we only perceive three dimensions of space in our daily lives, where are the extra ones, and why don't we experience them?" The idea that physicists use as an explanation seems to be that the extra ones are tightly curled up. One of the metaphors Greene uses to convey this idea is that of a distant observer looking at a tightrope stretched across a chasm. From a distance, the tightrope is a one-dimensional object—it appears simply as a line. We know without moving closer that it's really a three-dimensional object, but that's because our entire lives have been spent dealing with a framework that contains three-dimensional objects in three-dimensional space. Observationally, it's a one-dimensional object, because the extra dimensionality of the rope is curled up tighter than our ability to resolve visually from where we stand.

If we ponder the postulate that spacetime actually contains ten spatial dimensions, and these curled-up dimensions are too small for us to observe, we might ask how small they might be. We don't know for sure, because we've never seen or otherwise detected them, but they must be smaller than our most sophisticated instruments can resolve. But as an exercise in visualization, what if the vibrations that physicists talk about when they're discussing string theory are shaped and contoured by the tightly curled-up dimensions, much like the manner in which the sound of the French horn is shaped by the curves and contours of the horn?

If that were the case, we could think of all the elementary particles, the matter particles and the force particles, as the different "notes" played by that universal instrument known as spacetime. In fact, some string physicists have proposed that we think of spacetime as the essential stuff of the universe. All physically observable objects, forces, fields, etcetera would then actually be vibrational modes of that "stuff."

DIPPING OUR TOES IN 19TH CENTURY PHYSICS

Since we have pondered the idea that the building blocks of what we call reality might actually be vibrational modes of spacetime, a natural next question is, "What is spacetime?" What it is that's vibrating in this description? After all, in our human experience, we experience vibration as vibration of something. Water waves are vibrations in and of water. Sound is vibration in and of air. Also, we can recall the physicists' efforts a century or so ago to explain light. Clearly, light is a vibration, with the attributes of frequency (color) and intensity (brightness) that we associate with vibration. At first glance, much like the interpretation of ocean waves being a vibration of water, we might think (and the physicists of that time did think) that there must be some physical medium, some substance that permeates all of space, that's doing the vibrating.

A vibrating medium that permeates all of space is actually a subtly different idea than the one in which spacetime itself is what vibrates. In any case, in this view, space just exists, and it isn't anything in itself, but rather a container for everything else, including us. And if something is vibrating, it must exist in and permeate all of space. We can and do observe light that was emitted from distant stars more than thirteen billion years ago and thus must have been something like thirteen billion or so light years away when that light was emitted. Historically, the medium thought to fill all of space was called the ether. So the ether, if it exists in space, must fill all of space, at least as far as the most distant galaxies.

If that's the case, the Earth would be moving through that medium, that ether-stuff. Now, if you're on a ship sailing on the ocean, and as an experiment, you sail the ship in the direction the waves appear to be coming from, the waves will approach you faster than if you turn the ship around and run with the waves. In fact, if we know how fast the waves are travelling over the ocean's surface, we could calculate our ship's speed relative to dry land by performing that experiment.

Similarly, we should be able to measure the velocity of the Earth through the ether, or whatever it is that's vibrating, by comparing the velocity of light emanating from a distant star at two points in time. The first of those points might be when the Earth is at that point in its passage around the sun when it is travelling toward the star, and the other might be six months later, when it is travelling in the opposite direction. Like our ocean-wave analogy, when we and the Earth we're travelling on are moving toward the star we're observing, light should appear to approach us with a higher velocity than if the Earth is moving away from the star.

But amazingly (at least it was amazing to the experimenters when those original experiments were done), there is no difference in those measurements. The speed of light as it arrives from distant stars and enters our eyes or our measuring instruments is independent of our motion relative to those stars (and of the star's motion through spacetime). With that realization, the notion of a substance called the ether became untenable, and light came to be thought of as simply electromagnetic vibration without anything being "there" to actually do the vibrating. This observation, that the speed of light is always the same (i.e., is independent of our motion, and that of the light source), was the first chink in the armor of what is now called classical mechanics, the body of interpretation we inherited from Sir Isaac Newton more than three hundred years ago, and that was based on abstraction of physical, "common-sense" experience.

OK, so perhaps we can explain the appearance of the physical world as a kind of multisensory picture we somehow paint for ourselves as we interact with the universe of vibration we perceive. We may well have gone as far as we can in answering the question, "What is it that's doing all this vibrating?" So now let's ask, "What's doing the perceiving?" Is it the human brain that is making the interpretation we call "the world?" If we were to postulate that the entire physical world appears to us as a function of our interaction with and interpretation of a vibratory universe, then the brain would be part of that physical world, and thus part of our interpretation as well. It certainly is for the brain surgeon or the person performing an autopsy.

In the next chapter we'll go back to the questions of what is doing the perceiving, what is it that's conscious of this interpretation, and who or what is asking the questions? These questions are an essential part of the inquiry into what it is to be a human being.

CHAPTER 4

CONTEMPLATIONS ABOUT HUMAN BEINGS

SENTIENT BEINGS

The dictionary defines the adjective "sentient" as "having the power of perception by the senses; conscious." It seems pretty clear that word applies to us. But what is it that has that power of perception? Each of the disciplines I've already mentioned offered an answer to the question, "What is it that's aware or conscious of all the sensory input and resulting interpretation?" The answers almost always include the word "Self," a concept I will capitalize in this section. However, many so-called masters of this subject matter have said that you can't speak about that Self; in fact, as I noted before, it appears that our entire linguistic arsenal exists to describe what the Self observes or has experienced, and not the Self itself.

Language was arguably developed for working with the domains of memory and observation, and not for the domain of being. In this chapter we will bear in mind the difficulty of speaking of the Self with language developed for a different domain. We will attempt to approach the nature of the Self by drawing distinctions between what it is and what it's not. I have encountered several of these distinctions in my inquiry, and I'll present some of those in the following paragraphs.

Werner Erhard, from whom I borrow the idea of distinct domains of human experience, referred to the distinction experienced during that special moment during his training when the Self is distinguished from the mind. When I arrived at that moment in his training, my mind instantly went on the defensive, calling the entire proceedings "evil." In that moment of revelation, as I now recall it, I (my Self) saw my mind as something other than myself, and I watched my mind casting about for a way to explain what just happened. It was clear to me, in that moment, that the Self and the mind are actually distinct from one another. In the years since that moment I have realized with ever-increasing clarity that the voice I've always heard in my head isn't actually my voice; it isn't actually me. Werner referred to that voice as "It."

Don Juan told Carlos Castaneda that there are two parts to who we are. He said that the "sorcerers' explanation" calls those two parts the Tonal and the Nagual. The Tonal, he said, consists of everything we can name or even conceive of. It is responsible for holding the description of the world in place, so that there is continuity and coherence to the world we perceive and act in. Our language is designed to speak exclusively about the Tonal and its doings, what he called "the human inventory." He said that the Nagual, on the other hand, is responsible for creation. It cannot be spoken about or described. It can only be witnessed, and only in the moment in which it is witnessed, before the Tonal has turned its appearance into another element of its inventory, another memory. According to don Juan, one way to describe what it is to be a "sorcerer" is to know how to get to the Nagual. Once there, the Nagual expresses itself according to the mood of the sorcerer, and its effects cannot be predicted. If the sorcerer is joyful, for example, its effects will bring great joy. The two parts, the Tonal and the Nagual, as don Juan put it rather dramatically, comprise the "totality of the being that is going to die."

Esther Hicks, as Abraham, also speaks of two parts of who we are. In her description, there's first our Inner Being, "who we really are," and then there's the part of us that's focused in this time-space reality. In her formulation, we humans are multi-vibrational beings, capable of resonating with a wide variety of vibratory frequencies, each of which carries its own thought process and its own mood. She goes on to say that each of these vibratory frequencies can be a match to similar vibrational frequencies in other people. We have the ability to tune ourselves to a "higher," more joyful frequency. This tuning makes us immediately feel better, and steady practice of this higher frequency brings into our experience people who themselves are vibrating at this higher frequency. At the same time, people who are still vibrating at the frequency at which we used to vibrate tend to either adjust their frequencies or disappear from our experience. As an aside, this is a first glimpse of the alternative explanation for people drifting in and out of our experience, of which I spoke earlier. It's a neutral explanation, without the obscuring layers of meaning we tend to add, such as "what a shame you haven't kept in touch."

Hicks's description of these two selves, the Inner Being and the one we generally identify with that's focused in a body and a personality, seems to suggest that we actually have two selves. I think that description is a bit misleading, but having practiced her suggested techniques and thought about all this for a while, I've come to feel just how difficult it is to speak of the Self, other than to say that the Self is what has the power of perception, which of course doesn't really explain anything. However, I will press ahead in terms of her explanation and that of Werner Erhard and see where they lead.

In this "Abraham" way of looking at things, there is a relationship between the thoughts we think and the way we feel when we think them. According to Hicks, when we are being who we really are, we think only thoughts that feel good. In those moments, we typically describe our feelings with words like enthusiasm, excitement, optimism, and so on. By contrast, when we feel bad, it's because we are thinking thoughts that we would never think when we're being that real Self. In these moments, we tend to use words like anxious, worried, and fearful to describe these feelings. In other words, if we find a thought, and thinking that thought makes us feel better, the practice of thinking that thought allows us to more nearly be who we really are, and it draws into our experience other people who are of a similar disposition.

As I noted before, one of my habitual thoughts sounds like, "I am insufficient in and of myself, so I need to get people to feel sorry for me so they'll take care of me." That's a thought that never fails to make me feel bad, and its premise—that I am not whole and complete in who I am, that I am here because I have to improve, or to be better, to approach wholeness and completion, or maybe just endure—is a belief that who-I-really-am does not share.

Let's now pause for just a bit of reflection. When we begin to feel who or what we really are, especially if we begin to glimpse the possibility of living a more and more joyful existence no matter what's going on in the world, it seems inevitable that we will wonder about the content of our collective experience. Why is there so much physical suffering in the world? Why are there people who thrive in the worst of times, and people who suffer in the best of times? I will consider these questions in more depth in a later chapter. For now, I would argue that, contrary to popular belief, it's actually not what happens to us that causes us to feel bad, when we feel bad. Instead, what feels bad to us is our *reaction* to what happens to us, the thoughts we think about what happened, and most of all what we think it means or says about us that "this bad thing" happened to us.

I remember Werner saying that the first thing we think when we feel bad is "something's wrong with me," or "something's wrong with you," or "something's wrong with it." By way of illustration, Werner went on to say, "We always think we're sad *because*..." In other words, I'm sad because *this* happened, or because she said *that*, or because they did *that*. As I said in my introduction, we human beings have explanations for everything, and that seems to be part of what it is to be human. We spin an explanatory tale around our feelings, as if we have to justify our feelings, or explain them to ourselves or others. Werner said, "Maybe I'm not sad *because*. Maybe it doesn't mean anything that I'm sad! Maybe I'm just sad!"

Another question that tends to arise in discussions such as this one is, "What is the meaning of life?" It was in the *est Training* that I saw that there is no meaning "out there." In other words, I saw that there is no meaning in any domain that is external to who I am and what I'm thinking. Each of us ascribes all the meaning there is, and we do it by means of the story we tell about ourselves and our experiences. As Werner used to say, "Your life is empty and meaningless, and if you don't get to that, you don't get any further." When he delivered that line in his training, there were a lot of grim faces in the room. Eventually, I saw that for a human being, the meaning of life is a culturally derived idea, as are related ideas such as having a higher purpose or devoting your life to a cause. I now believe that we use these ideas of meaning, purpose, and devotion to cover up and thus deflect our fear of finding out that our lives might actually turn out to be empty and meaningless.

Our lives are empty and meaningless…that's a profoundly distressing idea for most people. If that's true, what's the point of living? When we hear those words we try to imagine being empty and having no meaning to our lives. Most of us come up with an image of a black, joyless void.

The dictionary has multiple definitions for the word "meaningless." The one that seems most pertinent to the present discussion is "lacking purpose or significance." Following this trail leads us to the definition of "significance," which is "the quality of having importance or being regarded as having great meaning." Well, who decides what's important for me? And if we define meaninglessness in terms of lack of significance, and significance in terms of having great meaning, we're chasing our collective tails.

Werner talked about getting to "empty and meaningless" so that we can get beyond that. The next natural question is, "What lies beyond empty and meaningless?" and why does Werner speak of getting there? Is there such a thing as an empty canvas or a blank piece of paper when it comes to living as a human being? I will argue that in fact there is, but I have to cover some more ground before I get to that topic; it's higher up on the helix I spoke about earlier.

The tentative conclusion I arrive at from all this is that the world we think is "out there," the one we experience, is actually an interpretation we make of the complex mix of perceptual input to which we're tuned. There's nobody out there to pass judgment on us, or to tell us that our lives should have more meaning in them. Said another way, we always have a choice about where to focus our attention, and that choice makes all the difference. We haven't yet gotten very far with the question about what it is that's doing the perceiving and the interpreting, but we have encountered an idea or two about how to live a happier life.

PHYSICS AND PERCEPTION

String theorists speak of a universe consisting of vibration (i.e., vibrating strings), and Esther Hicks speaks of us as vibrational beings. Those statements made me wonder whether the abstract principles of physics can shed any light on our daily experience as human beings. Put another way, it got me thinking about what the relationship might actually be between the vibrations of the strings— or of spacetime itself—and the vibration to which we humans are tuned. We tune ourselves to a particular vibrational frequency by the habitual focus of our attention. Whatever we focus on, if we do it long enough, becomes a habitual set of thoughts, reactions, and responses. That habitual focus then tends to attract people and situations that match that focus. Our thoughts become reflected in our experiences. As Hicks puts it, "You get what you focus your attention on, whether you want it or not."

So now the question is, "What is the relationship between the vibrations of spacetime and our thoughts?" When I focus my attention on those two seemingly different domains, thought and physics, some interesting relationships appear. The first one that comes to my mind is Newton's Third Law of Motion, which, simply stated, is, "For every action there is an equal and opposite reaction." As an example, if an astronaut rides a rocket to work on a space station, and if he or she gives the space station a shove, the astronaut will go hurtling off into space (unless restrained by a tether, of course) whereas the station will hardly change its orbit at all. It's as if, when you push on the station, it pushes back with equal force.

And because it weighs a lot more than you do, it moves a bit and you move a lot.

Newton's Third Law of Motion was developed to describe purely mechanical processes. However, this statement of Newton's law sure sounds a lot like the pushback I experienced when opposing those who were in favor of the Vietnam War. Some twenty years later, in another political incarnation, I tried my hand at being mayor of my town. In the course of many long and contentious debates, I found the same principle at work. The more strongly someone pressed his opinion on some subject in the debate, the more likely someone else would appear with an opposite opinion equally strongly defended. In fact, Newton's Third Law of Motion seems to me to explain why all of politics is, in my view, ultimately ineffectual and frustrating. No matter how hard you push, no matter how committed, forceful, and articulate you are in expressing what you believe to be right, someone else will push back equally hard, and the pendulum will swing back and forth, left, right, left, right...

I also thought about the Second Law of Thermodynamics, which states, in simple terms, that the amount of disorder in the universe (referred to as entropy) always increases. That law was developed in an effort to explain why many physical processes are not reversible. For example, while is it possible, statistically speaking, that all the air molecules you release when you allow them to escape from a balloon will subsequently find themselves back in the balloon, we never see it happen in the physical world. Similarly, if you take a video of an egg falling on the floor and breaking, running that video backward will tell you right away that you're not watching a real-time recording of what actually happened. So this law says that having all those air molecules in the balloon is a more ordered condition than having them spread out all over the room, which is what you wind up with as soon as you release them. That sounds a lot like what happens to my house and the rest of my life when I don't pay it sufficient attention. Unless I expend some energy to keep things in order, they do in fact tend to get spread out all over the place.

True, these are rather mundane examples of a possible relationship between the laws that govern physics and laws that might shape our thoughts and govern our daily experience. For me, they're just teasers. So I hope you will bear with me; the helix will bring us back here again. In the next chapter I will relate two experiences, each of which radically redirected the course of my path through life. In the process they also transformed the quality of my life forever.

CHAPTER 5

BY WAY OF ILLUSTRATION, SOME PERSONAL MEMORIES

A PERSONAL STORY—MAGIC, OR
THE WHISPERING OF THE NAGUAL

Sometime in 1974 I purchased a new car in California and drove it back to Colorado. I was making a living as a musician, but just barely, though that wasn't a conscious issue for me at the time. The vehicle I bought met certain criteria, but fuel economy wasn't one of them. On my way from Southern to Northern California, the math was always in the back of my mind, about gas mileage, the price of gas, miles and dollars to go, etcetera. By the time I left the San Francisco Bay area for Colorado, I knew I had a much slimmer financial margin than I ever thought I would have.

I filled up the tank in Berkeley. I remember looking in the pipe as I withdrew the pump, seeing the surface of the liquid shimmering as I made sure the tank was full. As I headed east on the highway, my mind came face to face with the possibility of not having enough money to pay for the gas to get home. This frightened me badly; I felt the stress in my chest and stomach. The voice in my head, the internal dialog, was so insistent that I could focus on nothing else. I heard it berating me for having bought the wrong car, for living so close to the edge, for being such a rebel, and on and on. If I actually wound up running out of gas, so I thought, it would mean that I was being as irresponsible as I sometimes privately feared I was.

Even though I had no religious training, and even though I had never even thought of praying, whatever that meant, I found myself asking for help right out loud. I confessed my sins (i.e., the arrogance of my refusal to consider leaving the music business and seeking a "real" job, my insistence that I was right and my mother was wrong about my attitudes about money, all of it).

In the next moment I clearly heard a strong, loud voice that spoke with complete authority. It said, "Don't worry, Larry, we will get you home."

Immediately there was no dialog in my head. I knew that something profound had happened, that something had shifted, though I had no words to express what that something might have been. Driving east through California's central valley, I actually began to see the countryside, hear the sounds of the car, and just feel better. Somehow I knew things would work out, and I could relax and just drive.

Sometime later, I looked at my gas gauge. I saw that the gauge had not moved since Berkeley, and still read full. My first thought was something like, "Oh great, now the gas gauge isn't working. Now I'll have to keep track of how many miles I've driven; it's a good thing I have the information I need to calculate when I'll have to stop for gas." Sometime after that, I noticed that the gauge had begun to fall. I realized that I would soon begin my ascent of the Sierras, and I wanted to have plenty of gas before I did so. By the time I stopped for gas the gauge read three-quarters full. As I got out of the car at the gas station, I calculated that the tank was really half full, and I figured that while the gauge wasn't working properly, I could compensate for its incorrect reading. Ever the MIT graduate!

I pumped the gas, standing there still feeling some of the relief I had felt when the internal dialog had stopped. The pump clicked off, and as I hung up the hose I looked at the reading. The car had taken a quarter of a tank of gas, just as the gauge indicated. I looked in the pipe, and there was the surface of the liquid shimmering.

Everything stopped again. I stood there in a strange mixture of disbelief and complete trust. Using don Juan's terminology, I say that the world "stopped" for me in that brief moment. By this I mean that the normal flow of events and of interpretation stopped because my rational mind had no answer. I had the clear thought that I had just experienced something outside of the boundaries I had always assumed were dictated by reality, by the laws of physics, whatever. Looking back over almost forty years, I have no choice but to see that event as what don Juan called the "whispering of the Nagual," the part of us that's responsible for creation.

ANOTHER PERSONAL STORY—A DEATH IN THE FAMILY

I met my first wife, Christine, after I was kicked out of the band I had been a member of for five years. Though I had never before been fired from anything, I felt a strong sense of relief. I'll describe the band, its successes, and its breakup in more detail later. I had no clear plan for what to do next, and I moved into the basement of the house of a friend of mine in Denver. Christine was living in the attic. She was also a follower of Maharaj Ji, and we practiced the meditation he had taught us together, along with the rest of the people living in that house. I think we all considered it an unofficial ashram. Part of the discipline in which we were involved (in the language of that time) was about the temporary nature of our time here on Earth, the fact that who we really are had been here before, that we would come again, and that we were here to learn and grow.

After being with me for about eight years, Christine developed breast cancer. After fighting it for a couple of years it became clear that she wouldn't survive it, although I don't remember either of us ever acknowledging that out loud. I continued to live and work in the town where we lived, and she wound up in the oncology ward of a hospital in a much larger city. I visited her most weekends, and her mother came out to be with her and watch over her.

One of the last times I saw her, if not the last time, the "whispering" came to me again. I remember her lying in that hospital bed seemingly asleep or just "not there." I was gazing at her face, and suddenly she opened her eyes and looked into mine with a clear, penetrating gaze. I'm not sure I had ever seen her that "present." She spoke one sentence, "I'm all right, you know," and I said to her, "I know." With that, she closed her eyes, and I don't believe we ever spoke again. I knew I had just been given an extraordinary gift, a clear statement, a reassurance, that even in the context of a dearly loved person "dying" of cancer, all was truly well, even for her.

CHAPTER 6

A DEEPER LOOK
INTO PHYSICS

A reminder to the reader: I really enjoy reading, thinking and talking about physics. But perhaps you don't. If that's the case, you're welcome to skip this chapter. My purpose in including this chapter is twofold: first, it's to try to persuade you that our belief in the ultimate reality of the world, the "seniority" of the world with respect to us humans, is just not sustained by modern physics. And as a second, related purpose, it's to further expand upon the idea that using "common-sense" experience as a guide to understanding how the world (and life) actually work is really misleading. So, if you skip ahead, please take those two possibilities with you.

MORE ABOUT STRING THEORY

In recent years I have reacquainted myself with the abstract ideas that permeate the domain of physics, and in them I have found a rich source of insights into the questions that form the basis of this book. That may appear as an odd statement. I suspect that physics is never taught with regard to how it might inform the question of what it is to be a human being. But recall that I began my account of this adventure with the idea that what we see when we open our eyes in the morning is actually not the world itself but rather a description of the world. As the helix brings me back to physics, it's time for me to describe in more detail my examination of contemporary physics, particularly string theory, in an attempt to convey how much of a contribution it has made to my inquiry into this idea. For the following (admittedly cursory) description of string theory I am heavily indebted to Brian Greene, and any and all distortions of his wonderful explanation or of the underlying physics are solely mine.

First, let me describe the theoretical context in which the theory appeared. The two great achievements of twentieth-century physics were general relativity and quantum mechanics. General relativity was developed by Albert Einstein in his consideration of gravity and the behavior of large objects, such as planets, stars, and galaxies. The latter was developed by Niels Bohr, Werner Heisenberg, and many others to explain the behavior of very small things, like fundamental particles (e.g., electrons, protons, neutrons, and so on). Each of these theories works wonderfully in the domain in which each was conceived; "working wonderfully" means, in this context, enabling physicists to explain observed phenomena in those domains as well as to make predictions that are later experimentally verified.

But problems arose when physicists tried to combine the two theories in cases where their respective domains overlapped. You may well be wondering how the domains in which large objects and very small ones exist can overlap. Actually, when we speak of large objects like planets and galaxies we do so because that's where the force of gravity makes a difference. The gravitational force is a relatively weak force, and it doesn't play a significant role in the observed behavior of fundamental particles. However, lots of thought has been given to the phenomenon of black holes, which are very small (potentially almost infinitely small) objects and that, because of the huge mass that's been compressed into that very small space, produce very large gravitational fields, so strong that even light cannot escape. That's an example of the overlapping of those two domains. Another is the postulated source of the Big Bang, whatever it was that exploded all those fourteen or so billion years ago, wherein, it is assumed, all of the energy that we now see expressed as galaxies and stars was originally contained in a very small space.

Gravity is a relatively weak force? It seems that a force strong enough to bind the moon in a stable orbit around the earth must be a fairly strong force. But consider what happens when you stand on the floor. Gravity will "try" to pull you through the floor and on to the center of the earth. But the electromagnetic force will resist that pull by causing the electrons in your feet to repel those in the floor. And since you don't fall through the floor, we can conclude that the electromagnetic force wins: i.e., it is stronger than gravity.

So, back to the origin of string theory. In what's called the standard model of particle physics, fundamental particles were conceived to be so-called point particles, objects without spatial extent (i.e., without the property of size). As I said before, quantum mechanics works beautifully with point particles. But when mathematical physicists tried to reconcile general relativity and quantum mechanics with respect to those point particles, they found that the resulting equations made no sense. Every time they tried to use the combined equations to calculate quantities that represent various attributes of fundamental particles, such as mass, charge, and spin, physicists came up with answers that involved infinity, whereas measurements of these quantities never yield infinity, but rather discrete numbers such as ones would expect in dealing with the "real world."

It turns out that the whole point of string theory is to conceive of the properties of fundamental particles as applying to objects that are not point particles, but rather objects that have some spatial extent (i.e., have the property of size). And the simplest object with spatial extent would be a one-dimensional object, a line, or in the parlance of physicists, a string.

TIME AND SPACE

With that brief and (I'm sure) highly simplified explanation of the origin of the string idea, let's turn back to the question of whether strings are objects vibrating in space. To get to the consideration of that question, we first have to consider the more fundamental question, "What is space?" Our human experience suggests that space is one of those ultimate, unquestioned realities, along with time and motion. Sir Isaac Newton postulated those ultimate realities in his "bible" of physical reality that stood authoritatively for more than two hundred years. As we move about in our daily lives, we take space and time for granted. We don't think much about the ideas pointed to by those two words, we just use them to figure out where we are, where we're going, and when.

Walter Isaacson, in his extensively researched and wonderfully written biography of Albert Einstein, wrote of this revolution in thought as follows: "With his special theory of relativity, Einstein had shown that space and time did not have independent existences, but instead formed a fabric of spacetime. Now, with his general version of the theory, this fabric of spacetime became not merely a container for objects and events. Instead, it had its own dynamics that were determined by, and in turn helped to determine, the motion of objects within it."[10]

Sir Isaac Newton's ideas about space and time as ultimate realities stood for over two centuries. Then Einstein came along and showed those "ultimate realities" to be something less than ultimate. Consider these counter-intuitive examples: we measure space in terms of length. Einstein's Special Theory of Relativity, which preceded and eventually led him to his general theory, clearly shows that when observers in different states of constant motion (i.e. speeding past one another) measure the distance between two points—or the length of objects in the direction of their relative motion—they will come up with different answers. An observer on the ground will observe a ruler zipping by lengthwise to be shorter than the identical ruler he holds in his hand. And two events that appear to be simultaneous to that stationary observer will not appear so to the observer speeding past him or her.

---

[10] Walter Isaacson, *Einstein: His Life and Universe*, p. 223.

In other words, it seems that measurements of size and duration depend on the relative state of motion of the observer and what's being observed. We humans typically think of the physical world as being what it is, whether there is an observer present to take note or not, and we call that "common sense." But the Special Theory of Relativity tells us that our common-sense description of at least those aspects of "reality" is simply not correct. Admittedly, the discrepancies just noted are so small, at speeds that most of us have experienced, that we don't notice their effects. But according to Brian Greene, if the GPS systems included with our smart phones didn't take these discrepancies into account, the results we see on our screens would rapidly become inaccurate.

It seems, then, that space and time actually appear to shrink and expand under certain conditions having to do with relative motion. Does this mean that there are different physical laws that apply to observations made by observers in different states of motion? Einstein was certain that couldn't be the case, so he searched for laws that would work for all observers, or in his words, would be invariant with respect to relative motion.

GRAVITY

When Newton published his book about physical law in 1687, he left to future explanation the actual nature of gravity, and the specific question of how it is able to act on bodies across enormous distances. By the time Einstein published his General Theory of Relativity, he had come up with a new theory, a new explanation, of gravity. Isaacson quotes Paul Dirac, one of the giants of quantum theory, stating his opinion that this new theory of gravity was "probably the greatest scientific discovery ever made."[11]

Again, at the risk of oversimplification, here's what general relativity says. Massive bodies actually "warp" spacetime, and gravity *is* that warping of spacetime. Space, through its warping, tells mass how to move, and mass tells space how to warp. The classic way to visualize

---

[11] Walter Isaacson, *Einstein: His Life and Universe*, p. 223.

this phenomenon, described by Greene, Isaacson, and others, is that of the bowling ball on a trampoline. If you have a perfectly flat and frictionless trampoline, and you roll a billiard ball across it, the ball will follow a straight line. If you put a bowling ball in the center of the trampoline, the billiard ball will now follow a curved path, not because there's any force acting between the bowling ball and the billiard ball, but because the fabric of the trampoline is warped. If you roll the billiard ball in just the right direction at just the right speed, and you ignore friction, it will "orbit" the bowling ball. The bowling ball, representing a massive body, like a star, warps or distorts the shape of space, represented in two dimensions by the trampoline, and "tells" the billiard ball, representing a planet, how to move. So it's not actually necessary to postulate a force called gravity that somehow acts across great distances.

It appears then that our common sense, our collective rational understanding of what it is to be a human being, based as it is on our direct experience and the input of our senses, is valid only in a narrow range of conditions (i.e., those in which we find ourselves). Our common-sense understanding of the world we live in apparently represents a significant oversimplification of the way things really are, but without this common understanding we would have no practical way of using the world as a context or platform in which to live our lives. And finally, I suggest we should be wondering whether in fact common sense is just not reliable when extrapolated to explain who and what we are, and perhaps even why we're here.

In the next chapter we will attempt to peek behind the curtain, to see what might lie behind what we've all accepted as being real. In a nod to L. Frank Baum, is there a wizard back there? And what might that wizard have to do with us and with what it is to be a human being?

CHAPTER 7
REALITY – BEHIND THE SCENES

So far in this book when I have talked about reality, I have considered the concrete, or physical, sort of reality with which we are all familiar. But there exists a different kind of reality, which I'll call abstract reality. Abstract reality lies behind or underneath what we know. Now, anytime I try to deal with abstraction, I like to have a metaphor to work with; otherwise it's just too hard to wrap my mind around it. So let's use the idea of a film projector (even though there may now be a generation that's never seen one).

What are the elements of a film-based movie house? First, before we turn on the projector, we have a big white screen. Inherently, that screen has no content – it's just a place to focus our attention when we get some content going. Next, we have a light bulb that projects pure white light onto the screen. Now, white light consists of all the frequencies of visible light, from red at the low end to blue at the high end, that together make up white. By the way, if you want to demonstrate to yourself that white is made up of all the colors of the spectrum, affix a cardboard disk to a drill bit. Then paint pie-shaped wedges in each of the colors of the spectrum onto the disk. Now put the drill bit in an electric drill and fire it up. You'll see the disk turn white.

OK, so we have white light and a white screen. The last element is the film. The film allows us to project content (the movie) onto the screen. It does that by filtering out various frequencies of light at various points on the film and allowing all the other colors to pass through it. So the movie, at least its visual aspect, is created by a process of removing, or filtering out, some of the light and what's left is what we see on the screen. Now, if we were to ask ourselves what is more real, the movie or the film, I think one can see that the film is more tangible, more real than the movie. If the power goes off, for example, the movie disappears but the film remains. And the film represents this reality behind the scenes, as it were.

So the elements of this metaphor are the light bulb, the film, and the screen. The light bulb, with its white light, represents all possibilities. The screen represents what we think of as the world, the context in which we live, the reality we perceive. And the film represents this "one step removed" reality, which from our human perspective is abstract, since we can't see it with our eyes. We see with our eyes only the results of subtracting from all possibilities those upon which we are not now focusing. But the purpose of this chapter is to focus on that metaphorical film. If we want to understand how our reality is created, we have to talk about abstraction, the "film" that is one step removed from our reality.

To get started, consider abstraction itself. The dictionary defines abstraction as a noun meaning "a generalized idea or theory developed from concrete examples of an event." So in general usage, abstraction is a method of dealing with or categorizing those concrete realities, specific objects, and actual instances we experience by finding the general qualities or characteristics that they share. It's clear from this definition that the realities, objects, and events come first, and the abstraction is developed from these experiences. In other words, it's an after-the-fact process, occurring after those realities are perceived. I'll call those "explanatory abstractions."

Consider, for example, the notion of danger. Danger is an abstraction, rather than a concrete reality. Nobody has ever seen danger the same way we see tables and chairs. A child may be pushed in the school hallway or bitten by a neighborhood dog, or she may observe someone else having a similar experience. For the child, certainly, these events constitute concrete realities. The child may derive the abstraction of danger from actual experience, such as the push or the bite, and express it in the story she inevitably tells about that experience; alternatively, she may derive it from anecdotal evidence, such as when parents, who themselves consider the world a dangerous place, repeatedly warn their children about the many bad things that could happen to them and the strategies they might use to protect themselves. In either case, the child absorbs those stories into her description of the world and, through repeatedly telling those stories, comes to feel that the world is in fact a dangerous place.

Now let's consider another type of abstraction, arising from a different interpretation of reality, wherein the world we believe we experience, with its concrete realities, is actually a description that we've mistaken for the world it describes. This description was inherited from the culture as we became its newest members. If you look at things that way, what the world might "really" be is actually beside the point; all we really have to work with is a description of how the world behaves when we interact with it. We then come to rely on that description, because it affords us a way to get what we want and avoid physical and emotional harm in the process. More generally, it allows us to make sense of, and bring order to, what would otherwise be a bewildering and virtually infinite array of sensations and impressions.

If you use that possibility as a working hypothesis, you may come to see that so-called concrete realities are actually formed by a process wherein new events, new people, and so on are forced to fit into a pre-existing explanatory or descriptive scheme. I say forced, because we depend on our description of the world for everything we perceive. As a result, nothing new can be allowed to threaten that description. Therefore, it might be that abstraction, in this case an interpretation of what we can and do perceive, actually precedes and causes the appearance of those "realities." In other words, from this vantage point, abstractions lead to concrete realities, and not the other way around, and objects become objects through the process of interpretation. I'll call these abstractions "causal abstractions."

That's a radical reinterpretation of reality. I propose it not as a fact but rather as a working hypothesis. If it turned out to be a useful idea, how might it show up in our experience? Consider the idea conveyed by the word "possibility." Referring to the dictionary, we read that possibility means "the state or fact of being possible," or "the chance that something might happen or be true." In cosmology-as-usual, what's possible is conveyed as conventional wisdom. As a practical example that many people experience on a day-to-day basis, especially as of this writing, consider that in times of a less-than-robust economy it's often considered not possible to have a rich choice of job opportunities. Many people have looked for work in that type of economy and considered their lack of success ample demonstration of the accuracy of that judgment.

As I write these words, the world is said to have gone through about five years of this so-called less-than-robust economy. But is there really just one economy that we're essentially stuck with, that some of us seem to participate in more effectively than others? Is the degree of relative prosperity each of us experiences due to some combination of education, skill sets, and raw accidents of birth—or just plain luck? Or is it possible that there is no such thing as "the economy?" According to the viewpoint that the world is created by the process of interpretation, the economy I experience is the result of me viewing economic activity through the lens or window provided by the possibility, or range of options, which I have accepted as being real.

To flesh this out a bit further, in the context of the possibility that most of us have bought into, the one we inherited from our culture, there aren't a lot of methods of tapping into economic flows that simultaneously provide both adequate income and the personal freedom to determine how to spend our time. Everybody knows that you have to restrict the uses you make of your time and personal freedom to those that don't conflict with your job, if you're lucky enough to have one. That would be called living within the options that are dictated or implied by the possibility you (and your culture) have accepted as being real.

SUPERSTITIONS

I will introduce here a seemingly tangential notion, but one that will shed some light on this distinction about abstractions, and that is superstition. What is a superstition? Werner once gave a wonderful explanation of this term. He said "Black cats are bad luck" is a superstition. But "Black cats are bad luck is a superstition" is not a superstition. As he once put it in his inimitable style, a superstition is only a superstition when it's not a superstition. Someone who believes that black cats are bad luck may well alter his behavior so as to avoid black cats. Someone who believes that black cats being bad luck is a superstition is likely not to alter her behavior, because she knows that black cats are not actually bad luck. Superstitions only have power when they're not perceived to be superstitions, but rather when they're perceived to be part of "the way it is."

So how about the phrase, "It's hard to find a good job in this economy." Is that reality, or is that a superstition? Again, if you believe in the truth of the statement that good jobs are hard to find in this economy, then you don't see it as a superstition, and in most cases it will determine not only your actions but your experience as well. But if you believe that the statement is itself a superstition, then your belief is not likely to change your actions, and it may not even affect your experience. You simply accept that many people believe it, just as there are people who believe that black cats are bad luck.

Clearly, there are those among us who experience both prosperity and personal freedom as a possibility, along with the options provided by that possibility, on a daily basis. As a rather stark example, every time I drive up to Aspen and pass the airport with its usual array of private jets parked right next to the highway, I am reminded that there are in fact people who live on a daily basis the possibility of prosperity and personal freedom coexisting in harmony. There are people who thrive in every difficult economy, just as there are people who struggle in every good economy.

ABOUT NEW POSSIBILITIES

Werner Erhard said that a possibility counter to the prevailing world-view has to be declared by a human being as an individual act of creation. By way of illustration, he pointed out that not so long ago, "human rights" did not exist. Kings had rights, priests had rights, but ordinary human beings did not have rights. That statement led me to look up the Magna Carta in the encyclopedia. According to Wikipedia, in the year 1215, the archbishop and the most powerful barons of England forced King John to sign the Magna Carta.

The Magna Carta was actually the result of a bargain between nobility and the king, in which the nobility was granted rights in return for renewing the Oath of Fealty to King John, without which the English monarchy would not have survived. To force the King of England to grant rights which had not previously existed was truly an act of courage. That act, which became the basis for English citizens' rights, and later for American liberties, was an act of declaration the barons made individually to each other and jointly to the king, after they took up arms, captured London, and in full battle dress, took King John by surprise. One can argue that in that act, human rights (at least in the Western world, and even though initially enjoyed only by the landed barons) became a possibility, and with that possibility came options for self-determination that had not been available outside of that new possibility.

What actually underwent a significant change beginning on that day in 1215 was a story. The Magna Carta eventually forced King John to obtain the actual consent of a royal council (which eventually became Parliament a few centuries later) before levying new taxes. These events can be seen as points of inflection in the story people told themselves, their children and each other about the relationship between the English people and their government, and about what they might expect in terms of the possibility of self-governance.

Perhaps a more fundamental shift in the story people tell about who they are was the much earlier one in which a set of oral traditions was set down over a period of time, in what we now refer to as the Old Testament of the Bible. Thomas Cahill, in his beautifully written book *The Gifts of the Jews — How a Tribe of Desert Nomads Changed the Way Everyone Thinks and Feels*, argues that the story set down in the Old Testament reflects a truly monumental shift in the story we human beings tell about ourselves. Before that story came alive, human life was thought of as the playing out of the wheel, "A vision of the cosmos that was profoundly cyclical."[12]

Cahill in turn quotes Henri-Charles Puech, speaking of Greek thought in his *Man and Time*, "No event is unique, nothing is enacted but once…every event has been enacted, is enacted, and will be enacted perpetually; the same individuals have appeared, appear, and will appear at every turn of the circle."[13]

In other words, prior to the Old Testament, the story people (i.e., the Greeks) told of human life was of one perpetual repetition, in which each generation acted out parts that had already been performed countless times before. But the story of Abraham, Moses, and those who came after includes a completely life-altering innovation: the promise of better things to come for the people who chose to live by the Covenant. In short, the people who created this new story essentially invented possibility itself, and in particular the possibility of the future being an improvement over the past. In reading Cahill, it seems to me that this may have been the most powerful new thought, the most powerful evolution of our story that human beings have ever had.

---

[12] Thomas Cahill, *The Gifts of the Jews — How a Tribe of Desert Nomads Changed the Way Everyone Thinks and Feels*, p. 5.
[13] Puech, Henri-Charles, "La *Gnose et le temps*"

In the light of this proposed new cosmology, which says that what we deal with on a daily basis is a description of the world that we've mistaken for the world itself, we could consider that the world we experience is made, not just of abstractions as I suggested earlier, but of that particular class of abstractions called possibilities. I would further propose that all possibilities that have been imagined and declared are present in our world. That seems to me to be the way the universe works. All possibilities that have been imagined and declared are available to us because human beings have brought them into being. I should note that we are born into an already-established possibility, which don Juan called the "Tonal of the times," and which doesn't require an act of declaration to be present as physical manifestation. Unless the Tonal of the times shifts, however, additional possibilities must be declared by individual human beings to be available.

DECLARING AND CREATING NEW POSSIBILITIES

What does it take to declare a new possibility? This is an important facet of the effort to understand what it is to be a human being. Speaking a new possibility aloud, or writing it down, doesn't seem to be sufficient—think of New Years' resolutions, for example. Before we explore that question philosophically, let's turn back to physics for some images that may help to clarify things.

Recall the example offered earlier of the television that interprets an electrical signal and renders it on the screen and in the speakers as your favorite program. How does the TV interpret a signal that the cable delivers to it? In broad, general terms, the TV contains an electronic circuit that has a tunable resonant frequency. By subtly varying the values of certain components of that circuit, its resonant frequency can be tuned precisely to that of the chosen channel. In the language of electrical engineering, under conditions of resonance the vibrational signal in the cable *induces* a corresponding signal in the tuning circuit. Once that signal is induced in the TV's circuitry, the process of interpretation (involving amplification, demodulation, and transmission to the screen and speakers) can take place.

One way to visualize in a very basic manner the idea of resonance is to move your hand back and forth in the bathtub. If you vary the speed at which you move your hand back and forth, you will find that there's one speed at which you do so that results in a corresponding smooth sloshing of the water. Most other frequencies at which you stimulate the water result in choppy motions that don't build up into replicas of the motion of your hand. The architecture of the bathtub, how much water it contains, and so on determine the bathtub's resonant frequency.

How might we use the idea of resonance to illuminate our question about what it means to declare a possibility in a manner that actually allows that possibility to become manifest in our individual experience? If we use the metaphor of the TV that renders an electrical signal, we have to "tune" ourselves to that possibility so that we resonate with it. How do we do that?

Remember that we no longer have to do anything about tuning ourselves to the default, existing possibility. We did that very early in life by listening to and watching our elders and our peers and by incorporating their story into the one we tell about ourselves. In other words, we already resonate with the possibility—and the set of options it implies—into which we were born. So what we're inquiring now is how to tune ourselves to a possibility that isn't the one we were born into but that somehow calls to us. The answer relies on a crucial realization. What separates us from this new possibility is not that it doesn't exist. It's already "in the cable," so to speak.

In terms of the explanation I'm proposing, the barrier—for that's what it seems to be—between ourselves and a greater range of possibilities of experience is a contradictory belief. It's some generalization of one or more of those self-limiting sayings, such as, "If something can go wrong, it will," or "This is a terrible economic environment," or "There's too much competition," or "There's just not enough to go around." If you can accept that you are in fact a creator, an extension of the energy that creates, and that who you really are knows that beyond any shred of doubt, then the barrier between you and your experience of a new possibility is failing to realize that those limiting statements, which everybody knows to be true, are actually superstitions!

ABOUT BELIEF

What is the nature of belief? And what is the relationship between beliefs and thoughts? The dictionary defines belief as "confidence in the truth or existence of something not immediately suscep-tible to rigorous proof." For many people, a belief in a Devine Being is an example of something that fits that definition. But what about "We live in a terrible economic climate"? That idea qualifies as a belief, but it doesn't fit the dictionary definition which requires that it not be susceptible to rigorous proof. In fact, of that belief about the economy, proof abounds! If you believe that you live in bad economic times, you see evidence of that everywhere. I would argue that the dictionary definition of the word belief is part of the old cosmology. In the old cosmology, the world is real, we have no choice but to deal with it as it is, and our beliefs represent our best efforts at classifying and organizing what we recognize to be true.

As part of our effort to understand what a new cosmology might entail, we need a new definition of "belief." I prefer the following definition: A belief is a particular combination of thoughts that have been declared repeatedly and long enough so they become self-evi-dent. "It's a terrible economy" is an example of that kind of belief. It's something that "everybody knows," and if you hear it enough times, you take it for granted, whereupon you see evidence for its validity everywhere. If you believe that you live in bad economic times, you really have no choice but to act as if it's true.

In this new frame of reference, beliefs are self-fulfilling. They act as filters, excluding all thoughts that don't conform to the belief in question and allowing only those thoughts that are consistent with it. So the relationship between beliefs and thoughts is that of context and content. Establish the context or belief, and the content or thoughts will conform to and continually validate the context. In this way of looking at things, a belief is actually a causal abstraction, whereas our culture has taught us that it is an explanatory abstraction.

The next question suggested by this inquiry is, "What is the relationship between thoughts and experience?" In the old cosmology, the explanation that most everyone accepts for why things are as they are, things just *are* the way they are, and we can have whatever thoughts we care to entertain about those things. According to that view, if we want to change the way things are, we can think about what changes we might be able to make, and then try to convince other people that those thoughts should be transformed into action. But what is the relationship between thoughts and experience in the new cosmology?

As a physics student, I became keenly aware of the so-called scientific method. That method, which has been the foundation of science for centuries, dictates that one first develops a hypothesis, then figures out what predictions one can make by assuming the validity of that hypothesis, and finally tests those predictions by experiment. If the experiment confirms the hypothesis, you're entitled to keep building confidence in it. If not, the hypothesis must be abandoned and a new one formed.

Can this method be applied to the relationship between thoughts and experience? If we look at the scientific method as it pertains to thoughts and experiences from the point of view of the old explanation, we have a problem right away. If our beliefs—and the thoughts that conform to them—tend to determine our experiences, then the scientific method will lead each and every belief-holder to consider his beliefs to be true and justified. Perhaps you've noticed that among today's "talking heads."

Werner Erhard spoke of the vicious circle, wherein our beliefs determine our experiences, and our experiences confirm and validate our beliefs, which serve to further determine our experiences, which more fully validate our beliefs, and so on. That conclusion is entirely consistent with the idea that what we call the world is in actuality an interpretation or description rather than the world itself. If you accept that we literally create the world through interpretation, then it seems easier to accept that our beliefs dictate the terms of that interpretation.

If we believe that we live in a difficult economy, that there is only so much to go around, and that jobs are scarce, then we will probably interpret every experience, and everything other people say about this topic, in that light. If someone speaks about his efforts to obtain a job, we see that effort as a struggle, and as to people who already have good jobs (or private jets), we say they're just lucky, or they just happened to be in the right place at the right time. If, however, we learn to see that a job, and the work performed and the compensation received, are actually physical expressions of the exchange of energy, and that the process of energy exchange is as natural to all living beings as breathing, then it becomes possible to see the effort to secure a job simply as choosing an appropriate place to tap into that flow. I'll discuss that idea further in a later chapter.

I suggest that our real selves, the ones that made the decision to be born into this time-space reality—as distinct from the selves that we invented to deal with the world's difficulties on a daily basis—are always present and available to us. And since our real selves, being fully empowered and completely free, never think thoughts that feel bad, we always have a reference point for how to improve our experience of life. We always have access to thoughts that feel good when we think them, because our real selves *are* thinking them. It's our beliefs to the contrary that generate thoughts that don't feel good.

WHAT IS THE SELF?

Now we come to what is perhaps the central question in our inquiry into what it is to be a human being. How could we think about the real self? Focusing on the word "real," does it refer to a better self or a different self that the one we're used to? Is it a fundamentally different kind of self?

Once again, let's see if we can go back to physics to answer that question. Every physics student ponders the question of what the universe fundamentally consists of. Most people probably begin answering the question by enumerating all the things they can think of. A typical list might contain matter, light, energy, and all the examples and manifestations thereof. If you're thinking from the old cosmology, which most of us do, that's a pretty good list. But the new cosmology I'm suggesting regards "the world" as a description. In that view, the world consists of the elements of the description (i.e., the abstract symbols we use to describe the world). Taking that view as a starting place, what could we propose as the most fundamental element, the most fundamental abstraction?

We've already talked about matter and light. We said that those facets of the world we experience are reducible to vibratory modes of Einstein's spacetime. What about energy? Speaking as a physics student, energy is an abstraction that we use to explain physical phenomena. For example, if a speeding car crashes into a wall, the energy of the car's motion gets converted into the energy of motion of the pieces of the car that fly away from the crash, as well as the heating of the air, the remaining pieces of the car, and the wall. One of the fundamental laws of physics says that energy is always conserved in every physical process. That means if you start with the energy inherent in the car's original motion, called kinetic energy, and you add up all the forms of energy after the crash, namely kinetic and thermal, the pre-crash and post-crash totals are always the same. Another formulation of that law says that energy can neither be created nor destroyed.

In other words, according to the way physicists conceive of the world, the notion of energy is *abstracted* from our observations as an explanatory idea. Certainly the most famous formula that references energy is $E = mc^2$. This is Einstein's powerful and often-cited equation that shows the equivalence of mass and energy. The energy in that equation is the energy it took to create a given amount of mass, and the equation's validity has been borne out by controlled and uncontrolled nuclear explosions. But where did that energy come from? Yes, the nuclear processes of fusion and fission release energy, but what was its origin in the first place?

Current scientific thinking holds that all of space contains energy. Even those regions that appear empty to astronomers contain so-called "dark energy."[14] Perhaps you could get rid of the idea of space and time, or spacetime, altogether and just consider that the universe consists of a boundless field of energy, existing everywhere and always, which in some times and places somehow congeals or condenses into matter, like galaxies and stars and planets and all the rest.

But now, let's shift our view once again from the old to the new cosmology. In the old cosmology we had abstractions as defined by the dictionary, wherein abstractions are "abstracted" from experience and investigation, and where the phenomenon precedes and suggests the abstract essence of the phenomenon, the underlying abstraction. In our new definition, however, the abstraction precedes and gives rise to the phenomenon. And now we must ask, "In terms of the new explanation, what is it that gives rise to the phenomena that collectively we call energy?" What is the abstraction that underlies and manifests as all the different forms of energy we can observe and measure?

Let's try the following, not as the "Truth" but as a working hypothesis: Energy is the only fundamental constituent of the universe. All matter is made of energy, and matter can be created and destroyed, which is to say energy can manifest as matter and then de-manifest back to energy. Energy is all there is—there is nothing else. But we exist—even those philosophers I studied in college accepted that. So we must *be* energy. Furthermore, we are conscious and aware, and we are conscious and aware of ourselves. So energy and consciousness must be one and the same.Simply by following this logic to its conclusion, who or what we really are must be conscious-aware energy. We *are* that which manifests as the world. Without us, there is no world. There is

---

[14] This idea stems from the observed accelerating expansion of the universe, which I touch on in Chapter 13.

no world "out there." And there is no "out there," except as a way to visualize, or interpret, the manifestations of the energy that we are.

OK, that's an interesting idea. Again, I propose it as a hypothesis, and in the sense that the Theory of Relativity is a hypothesis, it must produce testable predictions. For a scientist, observable results must follow that can confirm the theory. Can this idea, that we are all there is, be tested? Let's try to map this idea onto human experience and see if it makes any sense at all.

A study of conceptual (i.e., nonmathematical) twentieth-century physics has convinced me and most other scientists that the view of the world we derive from our sensory-based experience doesn't adequately or even accurately describe the way the world appears to behave when we study things that are either much smaller or much larger or much more massive than we are. In other words, the laws of nature we derive from our experience hold only in a rather narrow range of conditions. In our actual experience, for example, things don't appear to get smaller as they increase in motion relative to us; clocks don't get slower as they move relative to us, either. We don't see the very shape of space warping or distorting in the presence of stars, planets, or the moon.

The idea that what we call the world is in fact a learned system of interpretation of sensory input is very much at odds with "common sense." The dictionary defines common sense as "sound, practical judgment that is independent of specialized knowledge, training, or the like." In this dictionary definition, one is speaking of "sound, practical judgment" on the part of someone who has accepted the view of the world handed down to us by the culture in which he or she was born. However, if Werner Erhard is right, that our experience is conceptually based, in that our concepts devolve into experience and our experiences serve to confirm and reinforce our concepts, then the common sense that the "common man" acquires, "what everybody knows," may actually be worthless to an inquiry such as the one we are considering. That's because whatever we believe will turn out to be true; whatever our common sense tells us (and that we have accepted as true) will be validated by our experiences.

CAUSALITY AND "REALITY" – DIPPING OUR TOES IN QUANTUM PHYSICS

In the study of quantum physics, one discovers that the electron, the most commonly studied of the essential building blocks of nature, cannot be said to have a definite position or path until an experiment is performed to determine one of those properties. Well, right away we have a problem with common sense. How can an object not have a definite position in space? This apparent reality is not simply the result of measuring techniques inadequate to the task, as was first proposed, but is rather a verified conclusion—by repeated experiments—about the nature of reality itself. Bruce Rosenblum and Fred Kuttner, in their recent book *Quantum Enigma,* say that unobserved fundamental particles don't even have the *property* of position.

This realization succeeded in demolishing the dreams of determinists (I started out as one.) We had hoped that a complete theory of physics would allow the definitive prediction of the state of the entire universe at any point in the future if the exact position and velocity of every particle were specified at any earlier point in time. It also begs the question of how large, "obviously" stable things, like kitchen counters, can be made up of fundamental building blocks whose locations and states of motion cannot be said to have inherent, definite, and discreet values. Furthermore, our notion of causality presupposes that causes precede effects. But special relativity shows us that there is nothing fundamental about which event (i.e., the supposed "cause" or "effect") happened first; observers in different states of motion will disagree about those chronological measurements.

It appears that our common-sense notion of causality in physics is on shaky ground, because causality requires that causes precede effects, and special relativity won't guarantee that to be the case. Ok, but that's just physics. What about causality in human experience? The idea that "poverty causes crime" is a mainstay of liberal thought. Similarly, the idea that "welfare causes laziness and other irresponsible behavior" is a common conservative talking point. These are great examples of a human tendency to build a system of thoughts on top of an unexamined predicate or foundation. For us humans, the idea that events and conditions cause other events and conditions is so obvious that its validity need not be questioned.

But we could ask, "Does causality lie in the realm of objects and events, or does it lie in the realm of abstraction?" One big problem with the former idea is that causality in the physical realm is infinitely regressive. According to the dictionary, this phrase means a "causal or logical relationship of terms in a series without the possibility of a term initiating the series." In other words, if a current circumstance is said to have been caused by an earlier condition, then that earlier condition was caused by a still-earlier action or circumstance, which was caused by a still-earlier action or circumstance, and so on. At what point does the actual cause appear?

Now let's translate the question into the terms of the new cosmology. If we consider the possibility that what we think of as the world is actually a description we learned to perceive, and therefore the world actually consists of abstractions, can one idea or abstract symbol cause another? That seems to stretch the idea of causality to the breaking point.

Here's what I believe is an easier fit: it is in the domain of being, the Self, that true cause lives. Jane Roberts, who wrote in the 1970s of her experiences "channeling" a being called Seth, is said to have coined the phrase "You create your own reality." In my experience, when most people consider that idea they are instantly repelled by it. "Why would I create this experience (illness, poverty, and so on) that I abhor?" If it is true that we create our own experience, we must be making the choices involved in that act of creation in a more subtle and typically unnoticed manner than the way we decide what to have for dinner. And then there is the notion of victimhood. Are we victims of circumstances, whether of birth or of our own or others' making? Or are we actually victims of our own assumptions, our own beliefs?

POSSIBILITY AND ACTION

If we continue to pursue this inquiry into the possibility of living a new explanation, we will eventually come to the question, "What is the purpose of action?" If you believe in causality, wherein the conditions in which you find yourself determine your experience, then a primary purpose of action is to change conditions. This is another of those unexamined predicates that seems so obvious as to be invisible. Conditions cause experience, in the standard view. "Poverty causes crime, which causes victimhood" is one of the examples I offered earlier. Clearly, human beings use action to fix things that are broken, to make things happen, to change their lives—and, hopefully, those of others—for the better.

But what if we examine that foregone conclusion in the light of our new, trial explanation for why things are as they are? Our trial explanation for the way things are says that we are interpreting sensory stimuli according to a description that we've already accepted as real and that functions as a filter, allowing only those perceptions that confirm and validate what we already know about the world. Recall our metaphor of the film projector. The film in that metaphor functions as a filter, allowing only those frequencies of light to pass through and combine to form the world depicted in the movie.

If all possibilities that have ever been imagined still exist as possibilities, much as all the television programs that were ever broadcast are still propagating at the speed of light through the universe, what we're actually doing by tuning to one possible possibility is filtering out all the others. That's another way of looking at the function of a tuning circuit—isolating one possibility from all the rest.

But in general, any given possibility carries within it a certain, limited range of options. If I don't consider myself worthy of experiencing true financial abundance, for example, then the possibility to which I am tuned (the one I believe in) only carries within it the options called, "Keep this job because you may not find a better one" and "Get a different job because anything's got to be better than this," or something of that nature. It doesn't include the one called "Follow your heart and your passion, and you will wind up inventing, writing, or otherwise creating something that other people will find valuable or useful; do it because it feels good to do it, and abundance will follow." Recognition of that filtering principle implies that however much action you engage in, you can at best only trade one limited option for another one, all within the range dictated by the possibility you believe in.

So what is the purpose of action in an interpretation-based world? If it is not to fix anything, or make something happen that is beyond the bounds of the current paradigm, then what is left is to act for the enjoyment of acting, to revel in the sights and sounds of the world, to love being with and interacting with other people, and so on. In other words, in this alternative interpretation of reality, we really can act simply for the feeling of acting. This flies in the face of so many cultural dictates we can barely hear it. But it's enormously freeing if you can come to realize (i.e., make real for yourself) that nothing in our lives is broken, and nothing in our lives needs to be fixed.

I am proposing that everything we experience is an accurate rendering of our *view* of the world and our *view* of ourselves. Having a world of experience that shows up as a reflection of our view of the world is what I'll call a reflexive world. In that respect, the world we experience is a reflection of our beliefs, and the purpose of a reflection can be said to allow us to see ourselves, which is useful when shaving or combing one's hair, for example. Trying to change situations or conditions with action in the world, then, would be like trying to fix an unwanted image in the mirror without changing what's being reflected.

Imagine that you get up in the morning, go into the bathroom, and look at yourself in the mirror. There's a gigantic pimple right in the middle of your forehead! That won't do – you have a meeting this morning with an important person and you have a date tonight! So you get out your container of makeup, climb up on the bathroom counter so you can see really well, and you carefully apply makeup to cover up the pimple – onto your image in the mirror. Well, you haven't really changed anything, have you? And yet, if we live in an interpretation-based world in which the world faithfully reflects back to us who we've been considering ourselves to be, that's exactly what we do when we try to fix what we think is broken in the circumstances of our lives!

A PERSONAL STORY—MOM AND ME

I suspect that anyone who has grown up in a household with a parent who is a public figure will describe that parent as the dominant figure in his or her life. My mother and I were on the planet together for about sixty-two years. Memories and photos that I have from our early years together show us to have been very close. I experienced very little hardship in my life with my folks, unless you count the many, many evenings when, after having dinner together, my parents went out to work in the movie studios, leaving me with a kind, wonderful live-in woman whom I adored. From my current perspective, I certainly don't count that as hardship.

I did well in high school, I never got into trouble, and I was accepted to MIT for undergraduate work in 1963, just before Dad passed away. I went across the country for college, but Mom and I kept in close touch. She was devastated when Dad passed, but within a couple of years she had married another musician, to whom she remained married until his passing in 1987. I graduated from college with a degree in physics and went on to the graduate program that I mentioned earlier. My parents, Dad in particular, were left-leaning politically. They were adamantly opposed to war and the accumulation of money and power in the hands of a few. They were uncomfortable with intrusive government, especially in the bedroom or when institutionalizing discrimination. So when my interests and resulting focus shifted from graduate school to opposition to the Vietnam War, Mom and her husband were not surprised. I'm certain that her feelings were tumultuous when I left school, lived in a political commune, grew a beard, and finally escaped to the mountains, where I played guitar for a few dollars a night. I must confess I wasn't very sensitive to her feelings at that point, and to her credit she largely kept them to herself.

During my high school years, the first time I watched a rock band, on the black-and-white television in my bedroom, my Dad came in, got red in the face, and made a big show out of snapping the set off. The message was loud and clear. Classical music was obviously the only kind of music acceptable in that household, as far as he was concerned. However, I felt drawn at an early age to the electric guitar, and I spent years giving hints that I sure would like one. It never showed up, not until Dad had passed and I had graduated high school. Receiving that guitar as a graduation present felt bittersweet, almost as a consolation prize.

But there I was, in 1970, playing folk, rock, and country music in Aspen, Colorado. I had seemingly left behind an important, and certainly not inexpensive, education and career path. I expended enormous quantities of energy trying to justify to Mom (and ultimately, I'm sure, to myself) the choices I had made. I have difficulty reading the letters I wrote to her in that effort. I didn't bother to keep any she wrote to me, but she saved some drafts, and they're excruciating to read.

In the ensuing thirty-seven years until Mom passed, I never felt that she truly accepted me for who I really am. At every point in my journey through the succession of disciplines in which I participated, I made some attempt to share my ideas with her. She may very well have tried to understand where I was and where I was headed. However, I never felt that we had even begun to reach an understanding about what my life was really about.

During the last several years of Mom's life, my second wife, Kathie, a registered nurse, had an increasingly difficult time relating to her, but despite that, she wound up caring for her full time for the last several months of Mom's life. My relationship with my mother didn't end well, from the perspective of possible reconciliation with her before she passed. The last real conversation we had turned into a screaming match, with me doing most of the screaming. She was ninety-three years old, and while her mind was sharp and she was still able to get around, she couldn't drive and thus felt that her daily travels in the world had been sharply curtailed. I suggested hiring a car and driver as needed; it was clear in my mind that she could afford it and deserved to have the convenience her finances allowed. But what came out of her was, "Spoken like a rich man's son." Let's just say that my reaction to those words was neither generous nor quiet.

I've just related a story about a mother and a son. It has elements that many readers might find to be similar to their own stories. "She just doesn't understand me. Life would be so much better if she did!" I created that story. I fed it from year to year, and for me that story *was* the relationship. After her passing, however, something different happened that directly relates to the new life story, the new explanation I've been trying to explain in this work. In the course of many, many hours of reflection on that relationship, I've come to see what it means to speak of the vicious circle, where our beliefs determine our experiences, and our experiences confirm and validate our beliefs, and so on. I realize now that the story I told all those years about my relationship with Mom not only served to justify my actions and feelings but also served to perpetuate the "difficulty" of the relationship.

STOPPING OUR IDEA OF THE WORLD

The books that Carlos Castaneda wrote about don Juan Matus tell the story of Carlos's interactions with a man who called himself a sorcerer. There are "tales of power" in those books that relate incidents that a first-time reader might have a hard time accepting as real. For me, they're worth reading about even if they aren't real, because of Castaneda's skill as a writer. And if they are real, they're probably not much help to a reader who wishes to gain some greater degree of power over his or her own life, find some greater peace, etcetera. I wouldn't call those works self-help books, for example. For me, however, the value of his books is that while reading them I feel the "whispering" of that deeper Self that I actually am. For that feeling alone, I am very grateful to him.

But there is another idea that I take from those stories that is relevant to our fundamental question about what it is to be a human being. And it emerges from the realization that our idea of the world is what allows us to experience the world that we do. When it finally dawned on me that day in 1974, when I had no choice but to conclude that my car had just travelled a considerable distance without using any gas, something about the world stopped. Visually, it was all there; I could see the car and the level of the liquid in the pipe. I could hear sounds around me. I could feel the pump handle in my hand. And yet my understanding of the way the world works had shifted. I see now that what we call the world is a continuous, uninterrupted flow of interpretation. And in that moment, all those years ago, that flow simply stopped.

Castaneda related numerous experiences of similar disruptions of the normal flow of events. He writes that his first such experience, taking place in the Mexican desert, involved having a two-way conversation with a coyote. As don Juan put it, "What stopped inside you yesterday was what people have been telling you the world is like. You see, people tell us from the time we are born that the world is such and such and so and so, and naturally we have no choice but to see the world the way people have been telling us it is.... Yesterday the world became as sorcerers tell you it is. In order to [know who we really are] one must learn to look at the world in some other fashion [than the way we've been taught], and the only other fashion I know is the way of a sorcerer."[15]

With that simple incident with the gas tank, my now-decades-long inquiry into what it is to be a human being entered a new phase, that of learning to see the world in some other fashion, so that I might know who I really am. I don't spend time in the Mexican desert, and to my knowledge I have never met a sorcerer. But I have discovered that everyday life gives me opportunities to see the world in a different way than the way I have been taught. Because of the fact that I've never had a sorcerer around to guide me, I've had to learn to do this

---

[15] Carlos Castaneda, *Journey to Ixtlan,* pp. 299–300.

by myself, and it has been a long, slow process with lots of mistakes, and it has required a great deal of effort.

A PERSONAL STORY—THE PETTY TYRANT

This is a brief story about my son, Luke. I've coached him over the years in learning to see troublesome situations and relationships in a different light. Luke has a lifelong friend who in recent years seemingly missed no opportunity to criticize him and to pester him constantly about the choices he was making. From time to time I urged him to tell a different story about his "tormentor." To this end I used yet another idea from don Juan, the idea of the Petty Tyrant. According to Castaneda, don Juan said that the Universe itself is the Tyrant, because its reflection back to us of the description into which we live our lives is inexorable and unyielding. From the point of view of our new explanation, there seems to be no getting around the fact that whatever story we tell gets reflected back to us, and the conditions of our lives will not change until we tell a different story. Compared to the Universe, the persistence of the people in our lives who hound us is almost insignificant, and so in Castaneda's telling they're called Petty Tyrants.

Actually, you could say these Petty Tyrants are for us the personification of the Universe in a form that we can relate to as human relationships. At this point in my story, I begin to capitalize the word "Universe." That's because I now know it to be alive, aware of me, willing and anxious to lead me to a deeper understanding of my essential nature, and the ultimate expression of who I really am. I also think that Being, that so-called Tyrant, deserves a proper noun!

Anyway, let's go back to that story I told for so many years about Mom and me. I continued to tell it to other people for a while after she passed, but it felt increasingly uncomfortable to do so. Finally, there came a moment when I realized that to move beyond my feelings of resentment and anger toward her, I had to tell a different story. So I decided to say to people, when the subject came up, that she had actually made an enormous contribution to the inquiry that is the subject of this book. I said that without any hope of feeling the satisfaction of convincing her that I was on the "right" path and thus gaining certainty from her, I had no choice but to go deeper into the understanding of who I really am so that I could feel real certainty. So she became my Petty Tyrant after the fact.

That decision actually bore fruit in several different ways. First of all, I no longer feel the distress of the decline of our relationship. I think and speak of her with love again, without the guilt one might expect to feel from a difficult end to a relationship with a parent. And second, feeling all right with her again seems to have opened up the possibility of getting these ideas down on paper. I always felt powerless with respect to Mom, and that made me feel powerless in general. I realize now that large portions of my behavior patterns as an adult are simply continuations of childhood efforts to regain my power by resisting hers. I remember the dictates of Newton's Third Law of Motion, which is that what you push against tends to push back. Werner recast that as "what you resist persists." I'm no longer pushing against Mom, and I can feel the freedom that relinquishing that particular addiction allows.

RECONTEXTUALIZATION

The shift from tormentor to personification-of-relentless-teacher is an example of what Werner called recontextualization. Recontextualization means you don't change the circumstance; you just change the context in which you put the circumstance. I find that it works with memories, relationships, current conditions, and anything else that feels bad when I think about it. Recontextualizing my adult relationship with my mother turned her from a tormentor into a kind of life coach, like the coach who recognizes your potential on the playing field and won't leave you alone until you realize that potential.

The best part of all this is that I now feel my power returning. I can feel my power, my ability to live the way I want to live, to be who I am, without trying to please, without trying to be pitiable so that other people will feel sorry for me and want to take care of me. I can feel my power to express myself honestly, to be who I am in the world just for the sake of being who I am. And I can almost feel Mom "on the other side," cheering me on.

TELLING A NEW STORY

So it seems clear to me that to change your life you have to change the story you tell about your life. It's tricky though. If you tell a story that reflects the life you want, but you don't believe it, it won't feel good, and it won't change your life. Again, let's say you feel you don't have enough money, perhaps because you've been telling a story for a long time that paints you as a victim of economic circumstances or of insufficient education, or because you decided long ago that you could rationalize not having much money by considering yourself as being "more spiritual," or by saying that money is the root of all evil. Telling that story might in the short run make you feel better than not telling it, but it doesn't change anything, which reinforces your feeling of powerlessness with respect to money, and that doesn't feel good at all.

Now, suddenly telling a story in which you have plenty of money won't feel good either, because you know you don't believe it, and every time you look at your bank balance, you feel the same powerlessness all over again. So are we left with a slow, incremental approach to changing our ideas about ourselves, and about what's really possible for us, or are there levers available with which we can change those ideas in larger chunks?

ABOUT UNDERLYING ASSUMPTIONS—
"THE HUNGER PROJECT"

Let's look at a question that may shed some light on why it seems so difficult to change the story we tell about our lives, and that may as well provide a way to get a bit more leverage. If you were to finish your bathroom floor by laying large tiles on top of flooring that's not perfectly level, every time you walk on it, the tiles will shift. As a result, the grout that you so carefully spread between the tiles will crack and come out, and you'll have to keep replacing it (I know this from experience). It's the underlying floor that's the problem. Similarly, if you have a belief system that rests on top of a core belief that you never examine, it's really hard to alter the belief system because any new thoughts that conflict with that core belief won't be stable; they won't become new habits of thought.

In 1977, Werner Erhard founded an organization called the Hunger Project. The purpose of that project was to create "the possibility of the end of hunger in twenty years." He said then that the point of leverage over the human experience of hunger wasn't so much better agriculture, better distribution, or ever better political structures to make sure food was available where it had not been before. Rather, the point of leverage each human being has is the examination of "the unconscious, unexamined assumptions and beliefs that limit and shape our response to hunger and starvation."

Werner said, "The first component you see in the structure of beliefs through which we perceive the world is the component of scarcity. Human beings don't necessarily think *that* things are scarce. They always think *from* a condition of scarcity.

"For instance, while you and I might never have had the thought, 'Love is scarce,' it is obvious if we examine our behavior that we are 'coming from' scarcity with respect to love. We often act as if we must dole it out carefully and only to those people who deserve it. Also, because we assume that everything of value in life is scarce, we act to protect things—regardless of how much we actually have—because they are 'scarce.'"

Erhard cited another example of unexamined assumptions and beliefs that underlie much of the way we think about problems we would like to solve. "The second component you will find when you begin to look into the condition through which you are perceiving the problem of hunger and starvation is that of inevitability. As an analogy, suppose I told you that you could go through the rest of your life without ever having another argument. Try to put that into your structure of beliefs. Everyone knows that you can't not argue. Arguments are inevitable.

"It's not true that things are inevitable. What is true is that we perceive the world through...an unconscious, unexamined structure of beliefs that has a component called inevitability."[16]

AN EXAMPLE FROM OUR COLLECTIVE
EXPERIENCE—THE FINANCIAL CRASH OF 2008

The financial crash of 2008 provides a great example of a facet of the world in which we can see the effect of belief on what people experience in their lives. In their book, *13 Bankers*, Simon Johnson and James Kwak suggest that in choosing to "rescue" the big banks during this crisis, government officials acted from the belief that the United States needs the strongest (i.e., the largest) possible financial system to weather the storms of the ebbs and flows of confidence. Yet even a cursory analysis of economics reveals that the financial system's well-being depends entirely on whether most people believe that things are going well and that they will continue to go well in the future. People in charge of a system that depends almost entirely on belief (i.e., on the expectation of what will and will not happen) felt compelled by another belief—that it needs to be made bigger to avoid failure—to try to safeguard that system in a way that wound up making the damage that much more widespread and far-reaching when the system did fail.

As Johnson and Kwak point out, over the preceding twenty years, finance had changed in the public eye from a boring and slightly untrustworthy pursuit to the "glistening centerpiece of the modern American economy. The positive image of Wall Street had at least three main components. The first was the idea that financial innovation, like technological innovation, was necessarily good. The second was the idea that complex financial transactions served the noble purpose of helping ordinary Americans buy houses. The third was that

---

[16] Werner Erhard, *An Idea Whose Time Has Come*, pp. 5–6.

Wall Street was the most exciting place to be at the turn of the new millennium."[17]

"Financial industry leaders and analysts, along with government actors, built an ideology of the positive influence of product innovation. There were, of course, prominent skeptics such as Warren Buffett, but they could be ignored as long as conditions were favorable. We Americans (and others, of course) were trained by the success of innovation in the tech sector to believe that innovation was always beneficial and that that would apply to the financial sector as well. Armed with widespread approval, Wall Street effectively co-opted the ideology of the virtue of home ownership, which supposedly provided increased individual responsibility, financial security, increased community attachment, better care of property and structures, and on and on."[18]

Meanwhile the government became a cheerleader for subprime lending, Wall Street skimmed the cream off America's top schools and, among the economic and financial elites, finance became a highly prestigious profession.

This is a great example of an ideology, which is defined as a set of beliefs, values, and opinions that shapes the way a person or a group of people think, act, and understand the world. Here we have a belief system consisting of three principal beliefs: first, that we need the strongest banks we can get; second, that any of them would crash the system if it failed; and third, that we are so smart that we were able to create an industry that would replace the vanishing manufacturing sector in terms of providing value, jobs, and revenue. And of course, underneath all that, and almost never considered, is the belief—an arguably arrogant belief—that we are smart enough to figure out how to manage a system that in its enormous complexity is probably only marginally better understood than quantum mechanics.

---

[17] Johnson and Kwak, *13 Bankers*, pp. 104–105.
[18] Ibid., p. 109.

Speaking of quantum mechanics, in the next chapter I will argue the proposition that this foundational theory of physics demonstrates convincingly that there is no real world "out there" and that it (the world) therefore cannot serve as the context in which our experience takes place. It seems to me that our entire worldview as human beings is based on the assumption that our existence is held or contained by a larger context that we call the world. If we were to rule out the world as what contains us and everything else, what might we call upon to replace the world as the context in which everything else exists?

CHAPTER 8

LESSONS FROM QUANTUM PHYSICS

A note to the reader: once again, as in Chapter 6, if you want to skip this chapter, which focuses heavily on physics, please feel free to do that. But take with you the following conclusion: our common sense understanding of the world starts with the unexamined assumption that there is a world out there whether we're here to perceive it or not. And quantum physics, the most successful theory we've ever developed to help us understand the world, says that that assumption is simply not sustained by the facts.

Before you skip over the physics, however, I'd like to add one more thought (and a few more paragraphs.) It goes without saying that we live in a technological age, wherein at least some of the world's population benefits enormously from material advances that would have been literally unthinkable without an increasingly improved understanding of how the world works, i.e. how it behaves when we interact with it.

One could easily argue that one of our era's most useful devices, the smart phone, came into being as a possibility when our then-common understanding got "unstuck" from the idea that everything visible in the sky goes around the earth. Prior to the age of Copernicus and

Galileo, everybody knew that the earth was the center of the universe. But the global positioning system and many other aspects of modern communications depend on satellites launched into orbits. And these orbits could not have been calculated, let alone attained, without Newton's theory of gravity. And that theory, in turn, would have been unthinkable without the understanding that the sun, not the earth, is the center of the solar system. So I often wonder: why have the ideas that underlie quantum physics been so completely under-appreciated by our modern culture, even of those who constitute its scientific forefront?

Anyway… It is apparent to me that our belief systems ultimately rest on the assumption that we are temporary visitors in a universe that's permanent, and that the physical world is senior to us in that it exists as it appears to us, whether or not there is anyone or anything around to perceive it. It seems to me that modern physics has shown that proposition to be patently false. In Chapter 7, I described the manner in which special relativity showed that our common-sense ideas of space and time as fixed, contextual containers is simply wrong. It turns out that they are dynamic elements of our observed reality, changing in accord with the perspective (i.e., relative motion) of the observer and the event under observation. We now turn our attention to our ideas of the physical world in light of what quantum physics has to say.

Earlier we referred to the idea that a fundamental particle like the electron cannot be said to have a specific position or velocity until an experiment is performed to determine one of those quantities, and even then there is always uncertainty in any attempt to specify those quantities (as summarized in the Heisenberg Uncertainty Principle[19]). Let's flesh that out a bit more. I want to try to show more clearly that the belief in a world that exists independently of its perception, and therefore independently of us, cannot be sustained in the face of hard physical evidence.

---

[19] The Heisenberg Uncertainty Principle states that in physics there exist pairs of measurable quantities wherein the more precisely you ascertain the value of one element of the pair, the less you can know about the other. One of these pairs is the location and the velocity of a fundamental particle.

Quantum mechanics is one of the foundational theories of physics, and thus a basis of our attempts to understand the physical world. It is believed to be a complete theory, though that completeness was vigorously challenged by no less an authority than Albert Einstein, who spent much of the latter portion of his life trying to show that there has to be more to say about the world than what quantum theory says about it. Notwithstanding his efforts, not only is quantum mechanics now believed to be a complete theory, it also has the distinction of having predicted many experimental outcomes, none of which have ever been proven wrong.

Discussions such as this one usually start with the famous double-slit experiment with which it was proved that light exhibits wave-like characteristics. Referring to Figure 1 below, it has long been well known that water waves, if made to impinge on a barrier containing two slits, will cause two sets of waves to appear on the far side of the barrier, each emanating from a different slit. Those two sets of waves will create so-called standing waves where at some points the waves will add together and produce larger crests than if one slit is covered (darker areas in Figure 1), and there will be other points where the waves will cancel and produce no crests at all (lighter areas in Figure 1). The interaction between the two sets of waves is called interference, and the pattern they produce is called an interference pattern. Observation of an interference pattern is considered evidence of wave-like behavior. When that experiment is conducted with a light source and appropriately configured slits and a target barrier where brightness can be observed, it is found that light behaves exactly the same way. So light clearly has wavelike properties.

Figure 1: Water Waves Interfering

Then, early in the last century, it was discovered that light can also be seen to exhibit particle-like properties. In fact, Einstein was finally awarded the Nobel Prize in 1921, not for his theories of relativity, which completely transformed the way we think about time and space, but for his explanation in 1905 of the so-called photoelectric effect, which describes light as consisting of "quanta." These quanta behave like particles, in that they have all the characteristics usually associated with particles, most particularly that they come in whole numbers. For a while, people asked whether light was actually composed of waves or particles, as in "What is it really?" Gradually discussion of that question subsided, however, and we just came to think of light as having those characteristics, regardless of what it actually is. And this description seemed plausible enough to physicists that they didn't stress about it.

Soon, however, physicists did find something to stress about. When cleverly designed experiments were done on electrons in 1925, the very same interference phenomena were observed. It is one thing to consider that light has particle-like properties. It's quite another to face the fact that electrons, which had been thought of as matter, as point particles with no further substructure, also had wavelike properties. In physics this is known as the wave-particle duality. It didn't take too long for the physics community to come up with a mathematical formalism that describes the propagation of these "matter waves" and by extension the behavior of these electrons. However, coming up with an intuitive grasp of what was going on (i.e., the wavelike behavior of fundamental particles) proved much more difficult.

What gradually emerged from this conundrum was the idea that a fundamental particle such as an electron *has no physical existence other than the equations that describe its likelihood of being found at any particular location in space.* In other words, you have only a mathematical description of an object, but there is no object independent of its description. The equations—due to Erwin Schrodinger (1887-1961)— that specify the electron's spatial location in terms of wavelike properties are now understood to represent the probability of finding that electron at any point in space at any particular time.

Note that this is not the same as saying that the equations represent the probability of the electron *being* at any point in space. It appeared that the best physicists could do was identify the probability that an experiment conducted to determine the electron's position would give any particular answer, rather than giving them the ability to specify where it actually would be. It's important to realize that the relevant probability is not of the electron having a particular location but rather of an experiment finding it there.

When Einstein received this news, he and others argued passionately (and ultimately incorrectly) that while the theory shows that we can't predict a specific location for an electron but rather can only predict the probability of finding it in a particular place, the electron in fact *must have* a specific location. Since quantum mechanics does not admit that the electron actually has a specific location prior to its being observed, the existence of that actual location would mean that quantum mechanics is incomplete. The idea that probability and observation were part of the "essence" of the particle was something Einstein resisted strongly and tried mightily to overcome. He summed up his objection to the probabilistic explanation for wavefunctions with the phrase "God does not play dice with the universe!"

Again, quantum mechanics says that we can't specify where an electron is going to be; the best we can do is write a wavefunction, a mathematical expression that specifies the probability of an *observer finding an electron* at any given place at any point in time. This gives the flavor of what I mean when I said earlier that the belief in a world that exists independently of its perception cannot be sustained when quantum mechanics proves its own validity in experiment after experiment.

Carrying this idea a bit further, we might now ask what happens when an experiment is carried out in which a specific position *is* determined for a particular electron (within the dictates of the Uncertainty Principle). Before the experiment is done, quantum mechanics says that the electron is conceived as having no specific location but only as having the probability of being *found* at every particular location. I'm using the word "every" in the preceding sentence to convey that even though the particle may have a very large probability of being found at some particular location, it has a non-zero probability of being found at every other conceivable location, including in some other galaxy. Mathematically speaking, there is no point at which the value of the wavefunction of an unobserved electron becomes zero.

After the experiment, we know where it is. So here's the tricky part: How does our observation, through the experiment, change or interact with the wavefunction? It seems as if observation causes the electron to pick one probable location from myriad possibilities and make it actual. How does that happen? I should note here that according to Rosenblum and Kuttner, the definition of observation from a physicist's point of view has to do with a very small object (the particle being observed) interacting with and affecting a macroscopic one (a measuring instrument or a human eye, for example)[20]. Interestingly, according to this definition, consciousness does not enter into the definition of observation at all.

A number of answers to this question have been proposed; each is referred to as an interpretation of quantum mechanics. The first, called the Copenhagen Interpretation (due to Niels Bohr and others), says that whenever you try to "see" a probability wave, the act of doing so forces the probability wave to "collapse" and take on one of the possible outcomes. The probability becomes 100 percent at that point and 0 percent everywhere else. When the experiment is over, the probability wave asserts itself again (because the particle, again described by a probability wave, doesn't just disappear). But this interpretation provokes more questions than it answers. Is it measurement, or is it perception, that causes a wavefunction to collapse? One could wonder whether it has to be a human doing the observing that causes this collapse. Or, as a skeptical Einstein is reported to have once asked, "Will a sidelong glance from a mouse suffice?" Once the measurement is complete, what could cause probability to reenter the picture?

And finally, when the math is fully explored, the equations governing the propagation of the wavefunctions simply don't allow

---

[20] Rosenblum and Kuttner, *Quantum* Enigma, p. 84.

these waves to collapse. So either Schrodinger's equations (which have been experimentally verified over and over) are wrong, or the Copenhagen Interpretation of those equations doesn't work.

Rosenblum and Kuttner express wonderfully another aspect of this "quantum enigma" that has to do with our concept of time, and specifically with our idea of the past as being something that is fixed and inalterable. Referring to Figure 2, they describe an experimental setup equivalent to a beam of electrons being split into two paths by a semi-transparent mirror. It is possible to dial back the intensity of this beam so that we can consider a single electron's path through the apparatus, resulting in this single electron (as a probability distribution) winding up in a pair of boxes (see Figure 2). The figure shows the incoming electron, represented by a wavy line indicating the wave aspect of the particle, two wave "packets" representing the splitting of the beam, and the presence of one of these wave packets in each box.

Before the experimenter opens the boxes, he doesn't know where the electron is. Quantum mechanics shows that the wavefunction describing the electron's position is now spread out over both boxes. That means that the electron has an equal probability of being observed in either box. And according to quantum mechanics, this probability distribution is the *complete description* of the situation. To enable observation of where the electron is, we could open a slit on the right side of one or both of the boxes, and have the electron escape from a box and affect a florescent screen, indicating its location at that moment in time.

**Figure 2: The "Pair of Boxes" Experiment,
Courtesy of Fred Kuttner.**

At that point, two different experiments can be performed; in each case the experiment is repeated a large number of times. In the first, both boxes are opened at once, and the result is that the two portions of the wavefunction (one from each box) will interfere with one another. Compounded over a large number of repetitions, this experiment will produce results (i.e., a pattern on the florescent screen) consistent with the interference pattern described earlier (wavelike behavior). But these results *don't tell you which box the electron was actually in.*

In the second experiment, one box or the other is opened first. This time the result is that the electron will be found to be either in one box or the other, and no interference pattern is observed (particle-like behavior). Here we see that the choice of which experiment to perform affects the outcome (i.e., whether we observe wavelike or particle-like behavior).

That has profound implications for our notion of the linear concept of time. Since the observed position of the particle is associated with the path it took to get there (i.e., via an interference pattern or not), our choice of experiments affects the past! Rosenblum and Kuttner put it as follows: "Finding an atom in a single box means the whole atom came to that box on a particular *single* path after its earlier encounter with the semi-transparent mirror. Choosing an interference experiment would establish a *different* history: that aspects of the atom came on *two* paths to *both* boxes after its earlier encounter with the mirror. The creation of past history is even more counterintuitive than the creation of a present situation,"[21] referring to the experimentally verified fact that observation is what causes the outcome of an experiment.

There is one more aspect of quantum physics that I think shows how the independent existence of the world doesn't hold up. It's what is called quantum entanglement. From Wikipedia, "Quantum entanglement occurs when particles such as photons, electrons…and even [larger objects such as] small diamonds interact physically and then become separated; the type of interaction is such that each resulting member of a pair is properly described by the same quantum mechan-

---

[21] Rosenblum and Kuttner, *Quantum* Enigma, pp. 90-96. Italics in the original.

ical description (state), which is indefinite in terms of important factors such as position, momentum, spin, polarization, etcetera."[22]

In regular old English, this means that once separate entities (two photons, for example) interact and become "entangled," and are then allowed to separate, even by large distances, an experiment to measure one of those factors (spin, momentum, etcetera) that yields a discrete result for one of the entities will determine the result of an equivalent experiment done on the other, even though after their interaction they may have been separated by enormous distances. Einstein called this "spooky action at a distance," and if you believe that those particles are actually separated by enormous distances, you will have a hard time explaining how collapsing the probability wave for one determines how the wave will collapse for the other, which could even be many light years away.

In the next section we will consider another, potentially more workable and, I would argue, more satisfying interpretation of quantum mechanics. First, however, we will flesh out the concept of probability just a bit before we tackle another interpretation. The question is, again, "How do we get from a probabilistic description of the fundamental constituents of matter to the world we perceive?"

THE WORLD ACCORDING TO QUANTUM PHYSICS

The first thing to recognize about probabilities is that they relate to a statistical analysis of a large number of outcomes. This applies to flipping a coin, it applies to the deck of cards when you play blackjack, and it applies to measurements of various attributes of fundamental particles. In the first case, we know intuitively that if we flip an unweighted coin a sufficiently large number of times, the heads will approximately equal the tails. But with respect to any given coin flip, we have only a probability of any particular outcome, which is said to be .5, or half.

---

[22] http://en.wikipedia.org/wiki/Quantum_entanglement

As to the case of fundamental particles, if you take a lot of electrons and measure their positions and velocities, you will arrive at a statistical distribution of these measurements. That statistical distribution is accurately expressed and quantified by the wavefunction, which mathematically describes the probability of finding any given electron in any particular location. Since this approach was first published in 1925, experimental data have always matched these statistical predictions. Brian Greene says that quantum mechanics applies to all types of particles, not just electrons, and it tells us "not only about their positions but about also their velocities, their angular momenta, their energies, and how they behave in a wide range of situations, from the barrage of neutrinos now wafting through your body, to the frenzied atomic fusions taking place in the cores of distant stars....In the more than eighty years since these ideas were developed, there has not been a single verifiable experiment or astrophysical observation whose results conflict with quantum mechanical predictions."[23]

So now, let's state the problem—or the enigma—as succinctly as we can. When an experiment is undertaken to measure the location of an electron, you can think of it as one collection of particles, meaning the human and his or her measuring equipment, coming in contact with another (the particle being measured). Once you know the initial distribution of this huge collection of particles, Schrodinger's equations govern how this distribution will change or evolve over time. That's all you know before you do the experiment. But the experiment finds one answer to the electron's location, not a distribution of many possibilities. How does that happen? And how does the electron "know" which of those possible locations to pick?

THE MANY-WORLDS APPROACH TO QUANTUM MECHANICS

Our proposed new explanation for the world and our relationship to it says that the answer to this question lies in a unique property of awareness: focused attention. We perceive the world—and,

---

[23] Brian Greene, *The Hidden Reality*, p. 192.

incidentally, localize all the objects in it so that we can find things and don't ordinarily stumble over them—the way we do because we've been taught to do that. Essentially, we ignore all the other possibilities this unimaginably large collection of particles could take, and we focus on one possibility alone. In other words, we filter out all the other possible actualizations of the probability waves that our description of the world doesn't allow.

It wasn't until 1956 that physicist Hugh Everett came up with an alternative interpretation of quantum mechanics, called the Many-Worlds Approach. Everett said that "a more careful reading of Schrodinger's math leads somewhere else: to a plentiful reality populated by an ever-growing collection of universes."[24]

The idea here is that, rather than the probabilistic wave function collapsing into the "real" answer (to the question of an electron's location, for example), all the possibilities are actually represented in different "universes"; none are actually "realer" than the rest. So where are these other universes—the ones that correspond to different outcomes of the measurements whose statistical likelihood are predicted by the probability wave—the ones we don't perceive? Notice first that questions that begin with "where" imply a static, ultimate-context concept of space, the one we are taught when we're young. This concept is the one in which space is the ultimate container of everything else. One might also consider questions that start with "when," which presume the equivalent concept of time as a fixed, linear "something" that provides a container for events in much the same way.

If you start with the interpretation of space and time as the context for everything else, and you think of all these possible quantum mechanical outcomes as taking place within this interpretation, you get science fiction. If, however, you consider the possibility that space and time are themselves typically unexamined components of the description of the world we learned to perceive, then the answer to

---

[24] Brian Greene, *The Hidden Reality*, p. 222.

the question "Where are these other universes?" has to be the only possible experiential reference for space and time, namely "here" and "now." After all, a human being can only experience "here" and "now." "There" and "then" are completely different ideas; they are ultimately memories, and they can never be directly experienced. All possibilities for the configuration of the physical universe, then, are actually present here and now; our perceiving of one of those arrangements, then, is the result of focused attention.

Now consider again the dilemma posed by quantum entanglement. If "here" is an experiential idea, and "there" is only an idea or a memory, then one member of an entangled pair of particles can't be "there"; there is no "there." Said differently, "here" and "there" are not on the same footing; they live in different domains. I know that this sounds like a glib argument, like I've finessed the issue. But please, read on!

One way to think about all these possible realities being here and now is to remember that all of the television channels—and thus all the television programs—that are currently available are all here and now as far as the TV is concerned. In essence, they're all in the same location in spacetime, and our ability to distinguish one from another so we can watch a particular program is a matter of how we tune the TV. The very same thing could be said of all possible outcomes of an experiment to determine the location of an electron (and by extension, tables and chairs). All possible outcomes exist right here and right now. That implies that doing the measurement doesn't do anything to the probability wave function; it simply means that *in that particular arrangement of "reality" that we're experiencing*, that electron is either there—where you're looking for it—or it's not.

Is it possible to enter one of those other worlds and observe an outcome different from the one that appears so real? A science-fiction enthusiast would have a field day with that question, no doubt involving some sophisticated machine with a dial on it that allows you to select one of the other worlds. However, I think the answer is much simpler. We do it all the time! I suggest that we do enter alternative worlds. That is to say, we perceive alternative vibrational configurations that, when perceived, appear just as real as the one we're accustomed to perceiving. Most of those "other worlds" are very similar to one another, and we think the world we currently perceive is the only world there is.

On the television set I had when I was in high school, there was a fine-tuning knob that allowed you to perform very subtle adjustments to the gross tuning that the channel selector accomplished. It's that metaphorical fine-tuning I'm speaking of here. In our lives, we adjust the precise vibrational configuration as our mood changes during the day, and for most of us this tends to happen in response to life's conditions. When we do that, we might just make the traffic light we otherwise would have missed, or we just happen to run into a particular person who otherwise might have just left by the time we arrived.

I think it helps to visualize each fundamental particle (i.e., proton, neutron, and electron) as having some measure of possibility of being observed at every point in what we perceive as space, which is what quantum mechanics says. If you extend that idea to every particle that makes up what we conceive of as the world, so that every particle is in some sense everywhere, it seems a bit less outlandish that the world we perceive could subtly rearrange itself so that we see a slightly different configuration of physical objects and events. Right at this point I can hear the rising skeptics' chorus. "Here we go with some airy-fairy, metaphysical, spiritual detour." I say that's nonsense. I am simply appealing to what seems to me to be a logical extension of the ideas of quantum mechanics. It's well established that observation is the critical factor in causing our physical world to appear the way it does. And for us, observation is really about perception.

What does it mean that for us humans observation is really about perception? Let's explore the distinction between those two ideas. To a physicist, observation is a technical term, meaning that the collection of particles making up what is being observed comes into contact with another collection, namely the human and his or her measuring equipment. Perception is different. In terms of the traditional explanation for the world, perception is "the process of using the senses to acquire information about the surrounding environment"[25]. In the proposed new explanation for the world, perception is the process of using the description of the world to filter and interpret the complex vibrational signal to which we're tuned to render a stable, coherent, multisensory picture of the world.

Here's a substantially different way of looking at our ability to allow the world we perceive to shift. I have noticed in my own experience that making the effort to change my mood or attitude tends to make the world show up for me in my experience differently, and in a manner that reflects the emotional change. Here's an example. Previously, I mentioned Newton's centuries-old observation that for every action there is an equal but opposite reaction, part of first-semester physics. I experience the truth of that statement on many winter weekends when I go to the ski slopes. On a gentle slope, I feel very comfortable, and I experience no resistance to the way the world is for me. I let the skis do the work of controlling my speed with graceful turns, my mind stays calm, and I really enjoy the ride.

When the slope gets steeper, however, I start to feel anxiety. I resist the pull of gravity. I fight gravity, instead of enjoying the thrill of submitting to its influence. My mind gets involved and tells me I better slow down, better avoid that suspicious patch of snow right there, and so on. I work harder, I enjoy the ride less, and I wind up having to ice my knee when I get home. Almost exactly the same thing happens when I get onstage to play music with my friends. When the song is relatively slow, I feel as though I have the time to allow what I hear in my head to travel to my hands so that I can produce those flowing chords at precisely the right time, with feeling. When the tempo increases, however, I have tended to tighten my shoulders, and it becomes that much harder to keep up. Plus, I require ibuprofen when I get home. In both of these examples, as I see it, I have resisted or pushed

---

[25] *Encarta Dictionary*

against the natural flow of things, and that flow has pushed back to the detriment of how I feel.

The point here is that in the new explanation for human beings that I am proposing, we are fluid beings, and we manifest in our experience a world that actually consists not of objects but of signals, of vibration. In this description of the world we perceive, all possible configurations of that world that have ever been imagined actually exist in this moment, right here and now, and the one we're experiencing right now is the one to which we are an *emotional* match. And when we shift from one of those possible worlds to another by virtue of a shift in our emotional state, nobody else notices that we have shifted worlds because The Universe, all-that-is, arranges each and every human being's experience as a perfect, effortless composite of those emotional states. In this view, our emotional state is the fine-tuning knob I spoke of earlier.

OTHER WORLDS IN POSITIONS OF THE ASSEMBLAGE POINT

At the conclusion of Carlos Castaneda's fourth book, *Tales of Power*, don Juan disappears, and Castaneda's narrative appears to end. When I finished reading that book for the first time, I assumed that was the end of the story. Yet he wound up writing eight more books that I know of. He goes on to describe numerous additional events that took place in don Juan's company. In addition, he provides several markedly different accounts of what took place in that climactic moment, the last time he saw don Juan.

What is interesting to me is that I think Castaneda believed that his original story was complete, and that he had accurately related all the events that took place. He writes in those additional books about his recollection of those additional events after what he calls a "prodigious effort." After recalling those additional events, Castaneda says they could not be made to stand in sequence with the rest of his experience. He describes those events as taking place in "heightened awareness," wherein under don Juan's influence he perceived the elements of a different explanation of reality, and his knowledge of the normal workings of the world became temporarily inoperable. For those of us who believe in "reality," those stories are strange...but I think they're somehow beautiful and inspiring.

Don Juan's "sorcerers' explanation" says that our experience of the world is determined by something he called the "position of the assemblage point." In terms of this explanation, all sentient creatures have an assemblage point that selects specific vibrational frequencies (he calls them "emanations") for emphasis, and it is with this selection of frequencies that we assemble the world we perceive. Furthermore, by selecting a different set of frequencies, the world each of us perceives shifts and actually becomes a slightly different world. For human beings, according to don Juan, the position of that assemblage point remains fixed during the person's entire lifetime. Yet it can be made, or rather allowed, to shift. In fact, with the silencing of what he called the "internal dialog," it will shift naturally to a new position in which one's understanding of the world changes. And according to don Juan, the ability to deliberately allow that point of emphasis to undergo a profound shift is what makes the person a sorcerer.

According to this story from Castaneda, if the shift of the assemblage point is subtle, new possibilities can be perceived, and new abilities can emerge. If the shift is profound, the world we know can be made to disappear altogether, and a different world can be assembled. His explanation for those additional sequences of events is that the memory of those events is encoded or encapsulated in the specific position that his assemblage point occupied at the time, and by moving that point (or allowing it to move naturally) to precisely that previous position, the forgotten experiences are recalled and in a sense relived.

This explanation actually enlarges the idea of the vibrations I've already spoken of. In the metaphor of the television I offered earlier, the vibration or signal is fixed as it enters the television, and we can tune it in or not. Now we're talking about a mix of vibrational signals that we actually add to or modify with our experience, a mix that carries the memories of an experience that can be re-lived when we tune it in again. If you ask where those signals are, the answer is the same as we gave for the location of the TV signal a couple of pages ago. They live here and now, in the domain of thought.

Many people believe, and many disciplines use the idea, that our memories are encoded somehow in our bodies. But in our new explanation of the world, our bodies are part of the description, part of the time-space reality we create through interpretation. And the reality we experience is determined by the complex assortment of frequencies, the thoughts and ideas, we're tuned to.

In a couple of those later books, Castaneda recounts suddenly recalling episodes in which he encounters people in don Juan's world who did not exist in his memory prior to that remembrance. It is particularly striking to me that those experiences seemed to him to occur "out of time" and that they could not be made to stand in sequence with other memories of that same time period. It seemed that Castaneda, under the influence of a "sorcerer," moved his assemblage point to a new position, wherein he was temporarily in a different place and/or time with people he simply couldn't encounter in his normal state of awareness.

At first blush, this story seems a flight of fancy, if a clever and moving one. Yet this possibility seems to me entirely consistent with Hugh Everett's Many-Worlds Approach to quantum mechanics. I should say that in my world, the probability of meeting up with a sorcerer (as defined by don Juan), or of demonstrably assembling a different reality, feels remote. But perhaps it only feels that way because of the constant barrage of messages from every possible direction that the world is the way everybody knows it is. In other words, those other possibilities are not gone; they're like TV stations that are not currently being tuned in.

Esther Hicks, speaking as Abraham, tells a story about Esther searching in vain for a very special pen. As most of us have experienced, searching for something special and not finding it is often accompanied by feelings of frustration, anger, or fear. The story has Esther searching every purse, bag, drawer, and every other conceivable place before just giving up, resigned to the apparent fact that the pen was lost. Finally, days or weeks later, when she had completely forgotten the effort and was focused on other things, she put her hand in a particular purse (which she had previously searched thoroughly, turned upside down, etcetera) and came out with the pen. A traditional explanation would be that she somehow just missed it. But what if, by relaxing and being at peace with the pen's absence, she allowed her assemblage point to move ever so slightly to a position that also contained the pen's vibration or emanation?

In my life I have observed, through the practice of quieting the internal dialog, the noise dying down and other possibilities becoming visible. Again referring to my gas-mileage story, I believe that in asking the Universe for help (or whatever it was that I was really doing) and actually getting some kind of verbal answer (wherever that answer might have been coming from), I surrendered or relinquished the problem, the noise died down, and a completely unexpected possibility showed up, one that was simply not explicable by the laws of physics as I know them and that furthermore was manifested by a power not constrained by those laws. That power is in accord with don Juan's description of the Nagual, and I am left with the certainty that it lies dormant within me and within all of us.

CHAPTER 9

TOWARD A NEW EPISTEMOLOGY

Let's take another look now at what we as human beings *can know*. First, I return to my statement from years ago that you can never really know about the essence of something but only about how it behaves, or how it interacts with your senses, and how you observe it. I hadn't yet read Hume, but it sounds similar to what he said, which is that "Humans have knowledge only of things they directly experience." But what limits what we can directly experience? Our culture has trained us to regard the physical world, the world we perceive with our five senses, as what's real. In that view, Hume's statement seems quite obvious. But now consider that "real" world not as an ultimate reality but merely as a description of whatever an ultimate reality might be. Now Hume's statement says, "Humans have knowledge only of things that are part of the description of the world they have accepted as being real." That's a very different statement.

Let's explore this possible reinterpretation of Hume. In the experience of the vast majority of human beings, things are perceived only if they fit into our understanding of the world, if they are part of the catalog or inventory of what is allowed by our description or the world. Things are only things (i.e., perceived as things) if they are part of that inventory. That's because the word "thing" belongs to the language of our human inventory, what don Juan called the domain of the Tonal. If something comes to our attention that doesn't fit, it is either discarded, or it causes an enlargement of the inventory.

On that day in 1974 when my car ran for miles without using any gas, something occurred that didn't fit into my inventory of possible experiences. It was not allowed within the framework of my understanding of the world. My current interpretation of that event is that I had already spent a considerable amount of time reading don Juan and working on quieting my internal dialog, and somewhere within myself I had accepted that the world might not be exactly as it seemed. So when I saw what had obviously happened, I didn't reject the event but rather allowed it to expand my inventory of allowed experiences. I will say that for a few minutes later that day I tried to rationally explain what had happened, but I soon gave up. That experience actually demolished my understanding of the world as a mechanical, deterministic reality, even though I didn't yet have a ready substitute, an alternative explanation.

So now, again, what can we know? If you come to your life as the typical human does, investigating the external world, learning to get along with others, making and pursuing goals, and especially relying on the picture you paint using the input from your senses as your explanation of what the world is, you will never know what anything truly is, or how the Universe really works, but only how it behaves when you observe it. If, however, you are willing to come to your ordinary human experience as an inquiry into possibility, and if you examine your experience for evidence that supports a new possibility, then you can glimpse what the Universe, and what a human being, might actually be.

I suggest that there is nothing we cannot know. We can know who we really are, and we can truly explore the magnificent physical reality in which we find ourselves, not only as a gathering of facts, which admittedly can be entertaining as well as useful, but as the temporary reflection of where we are at the moment in a timeless, unending journey. We can explore the world as real, emotional experience. But you can't do that from a worldview that assumes that you are a transient in a permanent physical world. You can't do that if you look at life in such a manner as to interpret everything that happens as either a blessing or a curse, and everyone you encounter as a friend or an enemy, as good guys or bad guys, as us or them.

In Castaneda's reporting, don Juan used the word "see" in a special way. Castaneda noticed that don Juan gave the word special emphasis, and he presents the word in italics when he quotes don Juan using it. I think Castaneda considered don Juan's use of the word "see," and what meaning it might contain, as perhaps the most mysterious notion that don Juan ever presented. I did too. Initially, we are told that don Juan presented "seeing" as the ability to perceive people as "luminous eggs," or as balls of energy; these "eggs" also feature a particular bright spot that he said represented the assemblage point, where a particular group of "emanations" had been selected for emphasis. This description certainly bears a strong resemblance to the so-called auras and energy bodies that have been described to me in conversations and in writings, though I have no such personal experience.

Later in Castaneda's apprenticeship, however, he quotes don Juan telling him that "learning to see" was a pseudo-task, and that the real issue is the quieting of the internal dialog. There I do have personal experience, having practiced some forty years. I can say that when one quiets the mind and allows the incessant voiceover commentary about everything we think, feel, and do to die down, a different, subtler awareness emerges, what could be called knowledge without language. This is a knowing beyond the accumulation of facts. It calls forth the use of the word "see" as in "Oh! I see!" It reminds me of looking at a picture of a champagne glass against a black background and suddenly realizing that it can also be seen as two facial profiles facing one another. The phrase "Oh! I see!" represents a subtle shift in interpretation, and once that happens, you cannot go back to the moment before you saw from that point of view. When that shift happens for a human being, where the world ceases to be what it was, there's no going back. It's what happened to me in 1974, and it's what Werner Erhard called transformation.

WHAT IS IT TO BE A HUMAN BEING—WHAT AM I?

We've been at this question before, but now we might have a bit broader perspective from which to consider it. In normal conversation, this question is usually phrased not as "What am I?" but as "Who am I?" The change in the wording is deliberate. When people think of the first question, it always seems to devolve into the second. The answer people give to the "Who are you?" question usually consists of personality traits, as well as physical, emotional, and mental characteristics, and a name. The answer to "What am I?", however, is a much subtler affair.

I introduce now one more abstraction to be examined. Human beings have a quality or attribute called reason, and as far as we know we are the only life form that has it. The dictionary has a number of definitions for the noun form of the word. The one I'll focus on is, "Reason is the power of being able to think in a logical and rational manner."

We humans think very highly of that quality, that power of logical and rational thinking. It seems to me that we continually pat ourselves on the back for possessing it, and we often think less of people who don't display it in a consistent fashion. Perhaps the apparent fact that only humans possess it has also been used to justify certain behaviors with respect to the planet and its other creatures. But what is rationality? Why do we have it? Well, logical thinking is most commonly used to solve problems. Continuing to press forward, I find from my dictionary that problems represent difficulties, as in difficult situations, matters, or people. And what is the definition of the word "difficult"? The dictionary says, "…having aspects that are hard to endure."

Now, surely, we're getting somewhere. Putting all this together, we find that a common purpose of logical and rational thinking is to deal with aspects of situations or people that are hard to endure. But why are they hard to endure? Let's recall our earlier discussion of don Juan's Petty Tyrant. Yes, you can use logic and rational thinking to get rid of the Petty Tyrant, work around him, defeat him, or maybe avoid him altogether. And if you try that, you can be the judge of how well that strategy works. If Newton's Third Law of Motion actually does apply to human affairs, whatever you do to get rid of the Petty Tyrant's harassment will actually cause him to stick around. Or he disappears, but someone else takes up the mantle. It's the whack-a-mole principle at work. Whack 'em down over here, and they'll pop up over there.

Or...you can appreciate the value of the Petty Tyrant, which is to show you that the story you've been telling about him and about yourself leaves you feeling powerless, and that the feeling of power-lessness is the real reason you're finding him hard to endure. Here's the problem: When you give away your power (over how you feel) to someone or something else, you cease to consider yourself to be who you really are. The way powerlessness feels is actually your innate guidance system at work. If you use the word "power" cor-rectly (i.e., if you're not confusing it with force), you will eventually have to acknowledge that who you are *is* power. So you can't actu-ally give away your power and still experience being who you are. Logical and rational thinking, when used to solve problems, doesn't actually work in the long run. And that's why if you get rid of one spouse because he or she has undesirable characteristics, the next one will very likely turn out to have the same undesirable characteristics. Only the name and the specifics will have changed, but the way you feel when confronting those attributes won't change at all, because you've given the power over how you feel to something or someone else, over which or whom you have no control.

Are there implications here to our question about what it is to be a human being? I'm suggesting that our highly vaunted reason won't get us there. It's the wrong tool for the job. By the way, should we get rid of reason if it doesn't work as a tool to solve our problems? You can't get rid of reason. It comes with the package. OK, why do we have it? I spoke before about the coping and survival strategies we developed as children in response to feelings of powerlessness. That suggests to me that we come into these bodies, and this time-space reality, with a survival mechanism that will hold us over until we remember who we are. When we do recover that awareness, we will realize that, a) we are eternal energy beings for whom survival is a complete non-issue, and b) we came here with great purpose and intention that will keep us here in physical and emotional well-being as long as we remain within hailing distance of who we really are.

I'm saying that reason is not the right tool to use into an inquiry into what it truly is to be a human being. To say it a different way, we can't know what we really are by thinking about it. Well, what other tool can we use to probe the question? Perhaps you don't need a tool, unless the tool you're talking about is one you use to train yourself to quiet the internal dialog. You don't need an explanation about who you really are. You just stop identifying with who you're not. The self you *think* you are is not something you are; it's something you have. It's ultimately a story you made up about who you are. And as far as I can see, quieting the internal dialog is the most effective tool for getting underneath it to who and what we *really* are.

Let's now take another stab at our trial balloon. Suppose we were to answer the "What am I?" question by declaring the following: I am pure, conscious energy, the only substance or essence that actually exists in the universe. I am a perceiver of vibration; everything that has ever been thought, every idea that's ever been had, every possibility that's ever been conceived, still exists in those vibrational modes. I am fully able to create for myself a physical world, a time-space reality. As I prepare to emerge into this world, I choose on an abstract level a possibility to explore. To that end I isolate among an effectively infinite range of possibilities a set that matches my purpose for this foray into our space-time reality. This choice results in growing a physical body with a particular genetic makeup and social environment that leads to a corresponding life situation in the world that I can live out into.

That declaration is rather abstract and not particularly useful if you think about it. If you think about the preceding paragraph, you're trying to reason out the true nature of being a human being, and it seems that one can't do that. What could be useful, however, is to propose that idea as a theory in the scientific tradition, and to see what the implications would be in living as if it *were* true.

If we were to do that, we should be clear about our expectations. I don't expect by trying out that explanation, by living *from* it, that the world would be freed of the constraints of scarcity and inevitability, for example. But I know that one individual human being can experience that freedom—and the joyfulness that comes with it—in his or her own life to an ever-increasing degree, because it is true for me. And beyond that, my own experience has shown me that the awareness of that possibility can be imparted to another, provided that the other person is an emotional match for it.

What would it mean to live life using the explanation that I've proposed here? First of all, let's be clear—I'm proposing this explanation as a possibility for the consideration of anyone who is interested. I'm not saying it's the right explanation, or the true explanation. My guess is that anyone who wants to try out this explanation will inevitably start by thinking about whether it's true. I said in my introduction that these ideas lie outside the scope of a worldview that we accept as being self-evident. They lie in the domain of Being, and I've also pointed out that our entire common linguistic arsenal was developed to get at the domains of doing and having (i.e., of actions and objects), not the domain of Being. In other words, you can't think about whether these ideas are true and actually get anywhere.

So what would it look like to make an honest attempt to test these ideas and find out if their adoption would make a difference in our lives? In Chapter 7, I referred to the scientific method, which some people consider to be the crowning achievement of rational thought. To summarize here, the method is to adopt a hypothesis and see what predictions that hypothesis makes. But what would it mean to adopt a hypothesis about Being, which in terms of this hypothesis, lies entirely outside of the domain of rational thought?

There is a caveat that we prospective scientists had impressed upon us when we were taught the scientific method, and that is that belief has to be avoided. If you believe something is the case in the domain of action and objects, you are at risk of misinterpreting the experiment. According to Rosenblum and Kuttner, Einstein believed that

"Even little things have independent reality, whether or not anyone is looking. If quantum theory said otherwise, it had to be wrong."[26] As a result, Einstein spent years trying to demonstrate the truth of his belief, and arguably because of that belief, he missed the opportunity to correctly interpret the role of probability in quantum mechanics.

In our culture's way of thinking about truth, something is either true or it's not, and if it is true, we either perceive it that way, or we are somehow deluded or not seeing things correctly. I find it interesting that Einstein resisted strongly the idea that probability seemed to be a fundamental part of the nature of the universe, rather than a function of our measurement of it. He believed that none of the post-Copenhagen interpretations of quantum mechanics was the "true" explanation. In reading Walter Isaacson's wonderful biography of Einstein, I'm struck by how close he was to coming up with a more workable understanding of quantum probability; it appears that his beliefs were all that stood in the way.

Once again, physicists are taught that belief should have no place in scientific inquiry. That caveat to the use of the scientific method is, I would argue, not applicable to an inquiry into the usefulness of a new explanation in the domain of Being. The problem is that for a being that creates its own reality, belief is part of the process. If you believe that money, success, or love is scarce, it will tend to show up that way in your experience. So to do the experiment, that of living life as if the explanation I've proposed is true, you will inevitably wind up considering the effects and implications of your beliefs. For members of our culture, an explanation is true when the world shows up and behaves according to our explanation. But for human beings, in terms of the explanation we're asking how to test, "true" tends to be self-fulfilling. As I proposed before, what we say is true is actually an explanatory abstraction that, in terms of Werner Erhard's vicious circle, devolves into a causal abstraction. To repeat his terminology, our beliefs about what is true tend

---

[26] Rosenblum and Kuttner, *Quantum* Enigma, p. 155.

to shape our experiences, and experiences tend to reinforce our beliefs, and so on.

In terms of this new explanation, each of us has our own "truth" at any particular time, and the Universe, or all-that-is, delivers to each the manifestation or reflection of his or her truth in a coherent, consistent, composite form that has nearly every one of us convinced that it's the one and true world we're looking at. To see that, to really *get* (or *grok*, in Robert Heinlein's wonderful term) that we had to be convinced of it as children, is to look at the world in a completely different way. I have feelings of awe and joyful appreciation every time that way of perceiving comes back into focus for me.

So what we need is a subtly different version of the scientific method, one that does account for belief. I'm suggesting that we need to put aside the criterion called "truth" when considering this way of living a human life. I'm proposing that the only value of an explanation about whom and what we are, and what the world really is, has to involve something like the quality of one's life. In other words, rather than being "true," an explanation about what you and the world are has to be useful; it has to work in the area of quality of life.

How are we to measure the quality of a person's life? It seems obvious to me that we can only measure the quality of one human life, and that's our own. As well as I think I know other people, I always know deep down that I don't really know much about their paths through life, what their purpose is in being here, and what is the reason why they came. Not being present to that apparent truth has, in not just a few cases, left me in a considerable state of bewilderment. "Why did she say that?" "Why is he acting that way?" Those questions seem to lead inevitably to "What did I do wrong?" It also prompted me to ask, "How can I alter my actions or words so that I elicit from her or him behavior and words that feel better to me?"

There's no logical way out of that mess of self-criticism. Like most everyone else, I grew up believing that other peoples' actions and words had power when it comes to the quality of *my* life, when it comes to how I really *feel*. When you look at other people from there, from thinking that they affect your happiness, you can't see them as who they really are, but rather only as others whom you have to manipulate or with whom you have to contend.

When I think about measuring the quality of my own life, however, things become very clear. I know when I feel good, and I know when I don't. There are many words people use to refer to feeling good: happy, joyful, pleased, thrilled, overjoyed, ecstatic, and so on. While I enjoy having experiences that involve feeling those kinds of highs, my preference is for the simple state of being at peace, of ease, of gentle flow. As I've thought about that state over the years, it's clear to me that that's who I am. In other words, it's the way I feel when everything else is allowed to diminish or fall away. For me, happiness is intimately related to peacefulness. If I'm at peace, being what I really am, what I really am is happy.

For me, that's the whole point of meditation. In meditation, thoughts diminish by degrees, only to arise again when attention wavers, only to be released again when one becomes aware that one's attention has wavered, and so on. As verbal thought, the internal dialog, dies down, I'm left with focusing my attention on just being, on just being aware. In those quiet moments I feel the peace I refer to. But over many years I have found I can also experience that peace whenever I maintain my focus on my actual in-the-moment experience (i.e., somewhere other than the domain of thought). I practice doing this while walking, driving, playing music—that is, when I'm just playing it, not thinking about playing it, how I'm doing, whether the band likes me, etcetera—and being with a good and trusted friend. I know in the depths of myself that I can experience that peace whenever I choose, but it requires, again, that focusing of attention.

To feel the peace I've just described, thought must diminish. Does that mean that if I want to be at peace, I can't have thoughts? Actually, it doesn't mean that. In the presence of thought, peace seems to be replaced by feeling either the excitement of certain thoughts or the discomfort of other thoughts. What makes the difference? The thoughts that I associate with excitement, anticipation, or just pure enjoyment are thoughts that are consistent with who I really am, in that they don't have components of limitation, scarcity, inevitability, and so on. On the other hand, the thoughts I find uncomfortable tend to arise from noticing that something is not as I want it to be and, out of habit, trying to fix the situation using reason (which is like putting makeup on the mirror). So the way I feel serves as guidance. It's very reliable guidance, as long as my objective is to be happy (i.e., to be who I really am). Ultimately, then, feeling good is like Hansel and Gretel's breadcrumbs, a trail I can follow to guide myself back home.

I know now that I came to this time-space reality with the power of preference. I can notice what I like and what I don't like, what I don't like is immediately noticed by my real Self, and what it (I) would prefer is immediately made available. After all, if you were a powerful creator in absolute control of your creations, that's what you would do! And I came here with the capacity of thought, and what I think, particularly what I habitually think, determines the quality of my experience. As I tune my thoughts so that my feelings are increasingly joyful, I become more and more the joyful creator I came here to be. And then my experience steadily morphs into my heart's desire.

So we have by now fleshed out most of this new, alternative explanation of the Being of human beings. What we think of as the world is a description, an interpretation of our sensory input. It's essentially a story. And what we think of as ourselves is also part of that story. Everything we perceive, including our bodies, and even space and time, is part of that interpretation. What are we left with to identify with? I suggest that what's left is feeling. Feeling is not part of the interpretation we call the world. The way I feel is just the way I feel, and it is the way I experience living in the world.

As I write these words, I am keenly aware that I have in fact adopted an explanation that constitutes a radical reinterpretation of the world I experience and my relationship to it. I often find myself switching back and forth between this new explanation and the one I grew up with, comparing how I feel when applying each explanation in turn to whatever experiences my life offers. In the next chapter I will describe several phases of my life. I present these events as pure data, and I will offer my current interpretation of the role they played in the evolution of my understanding and appreciation of the way they are all connected. Again, I don't think that as pure narrative my story is worthy of any more notice than anyone else's. I present it, rather, as an example of a life lived as a calling, in which I wound up abandoning the traditional notion of preparation, career, etc. and allowed myself to be led from one experience to another on what don Juan called a Path with Heart.

CHAPTER 10
LIVING LIFE AS A CALLING

A PERSONAL STORY—FORESAKING
ACADEMIA FOR POLITICS IN THE STREET

I enrolled in a PhD program in physics at the University of California, San Diego in the fall of 1967. As part of this program I was given a part-time job as a research assistant. The group that accepted me was engaged in searching for and analyzing evidence of stars that emit x-rays. To do this, an instrument package was developed that contained something called a servo-controlled guidance system. With this guidance system (at the time somewhat innovative), the x-ray detectors could be kept focused on a particular point in the sky. The package was then suspended below a hot-air balloon that was driven to a location in Arizona and launched to an altitude sufficient to allow observation unencumbered by most of the atmosphere. Subsequently, with the help of radio signals, the balloon was tracked as it drifted with prevailing winds to Texas, where it would descend and be recovered.

Sometime in the following year, 1968, I realized that I might be subject to the Vietnam-era draft. This was before the institution of the lottery system, which at least lent some predictability to the process. After consultation with advisors provided by Mom and her husband, it was recommended to me that the best way to avoid being drafted would be to find a way to fail the physical examination. My efforts in that area were to be two-pronged: first, to contrive a way to demonstrate debilitating allergies to the examiners, and second, to take the physical exam in some less-populated place other than California, where it might be more likely that an examiner would actually look at the facts.

For the first prong, I found that there were certain foods and certain pets, namely cats, which would make my existing allergies considerably worse. For the second, I travelled frequently to Albuquerque, New Mexico, where my family had friends, and established a history of work-related residence there in conjunction with the balloon flyovers. When I finally did take the physical, everything worked like a charm, and I received a 1Y classification, which put me behind all the 1A men in the draft order. In retrospect it seems like an extraordinary contrivance, costing lots of time, effort, and money, but at the time it seemed well worth all of that. When the lottery was conducted I received the number 307, which all but assured I would never be called anyway.

UC San Diego's Revelle College, home to the physics department, had academic buildings surrounding a central open space, called the quad. Passing the quad on my way to class, my attention was attracted to the discussions about the war in Vietnam that seemed to be taking place there at all times of the day. At first I was just curious, but by my second year I spent more time there than in class. The contrast between the two paths, studying physics and learning about powerful social forces, was striking. The former was a profoundly intellectual endeavor, while the latter took place on many levels, certainly intellectual but also emotional. I was excited by the passion with which people spoke about their disenchantment with American culture and politics. I was drawn to these activities to the point where I found it increasingly difficult to use the idea of "preparation for my future" as a reason for limiting my participation to those periods of time that lay between my academic responsibilities.

The incident that precipitated my withdrawal from the university was the People's Park March, which took place in Berkeley, California on May 30, 1969. For me, and for many others I'm sure, it was truly a watershed event. The context for that march was typical of the free-speech and antiwar movements of the 1960s. It involved a clash of highly symbolic acts: the unsanctioned improvements to university-owned vacant land near the Berkeley campus by student volunteers; the high marks given the project by area merchants; the tentative but quickly withdrawn decision by university officials to build a sports field there instead; and finally, the forcible and ultimately deadly destruction of the park improvements by a governor (Ronald Reagan) who had promised to "crack down on what the public perceived as a generally lax attitude at California's public universities. Reagan called the Berkeley campus 'a haven for communist sympathizers, protesters, and sex deviants.' Reagan considered the creation of the park a direct leftist challenge to the property rights of the university, and he found in it an opportunity to fulfill his campaign promise."[27]

I use the phrase "highly symbolic" to reflect the underlying phenomenon of action and reaction, of which I've already spoken. Newton's Third Law of Motion speaks of equal and opposite reaction, but I've noticed that in political affairs it's often asymmetrical; when strong emotions are involved, people tend to react out of proportion to the original action. Governor Reagan made his decision in order to "send a message"; his use of force seemed to me and many others highly excessive. According to the same Wikipedia article, "The police were permitted to use whatever methods they chose against the crowds, which had swelled to approximately six thousand people. Officers in full riot gear (helmets, shields, and gas masks) obscured their badges to avoid being identified and headed into the crowds with night-sticks swinging....At least 128 Berkeley residents were admitted to local hospitals for head trauma, shotgun wounds, and other serious injuries inflicted by police." One man watching from a rooftop was killed, another permanently blinded.

It's worth continuing to quote Wikipedia about the events that followed, as I was there, and my memories are entirely consistent. On May 30, 1969, thirty thousand Berkeley citizens (out of a population of

---

[27] http://en.wikipedia.org/wiki/People%27s_Park

one hundred thousand) "secured a Berkeley city permit and marched without incident past barricaded People's Park to protest Governor Reagan's occupation of their city, the death of James Rector, the blinding of Alan Blanchard, and the many injuries inflicted by police. Young girls slid flowers down the muzzles of bayoneted National Guard rifles, and a small airplane flew over the city trailing a banner that read, 'Let A Thousand Parks Bloom.'

"In an address before the California Council of Growers on 7 April 1970, almost a year after 'Bloody Thursday' and the death of James Rector, Governor Reagan defended his decision to use the California National Guard to quell Berkeley protests: 'If it takes a bloodbath, let's get it over with. No more appeasement.' Just a few weeks later, on 4 May 1970, the Ohio National Guard fired on protestors at Kent State University, killing four students and seriously wounding nine."[28]

Following our trip to Berkeley, these events were the subject of much discussion, and the passions ignited brought many more people into the community of war resistors. I had never before seen up close the phenomenon I refer to as "Us vs. Them." As I use the terms here, "us" and "them" are explanatory abstractions, in that they give us an explanation with which to grasp our experiences. They allowed us to identify our "enemies" and to gather ourselves together to fight them. We used words like "the system" and "the establishment" in identifying our adversaries, and words like "the people" to identify ourselves.

The trouble is, those explanatory abstractions have a way of becoming causal explanations, in that as one persists in dividing the world into "us" and "them," the world tends to show up in a manner consistent with those categories. We are provided with more and more evidence that we have correctly identified the good guys and the bad guys. And this evidence further reinforces the correctness of our categorization scheme, and once again we get to be right, and all we had

---

[28] http://en.wikipedia.org/wiki/People%27s_Park

to sacrifice for that rightness is any power to change our experience to something more desirable.

Back in San Diego, our response to this increasing polarization was to gather together in a political commune to create and publish an underground newspaper. Originally, we named it the *San Diego Free Press*, but later it was changed to the *San Diego Street Journal* as we became more militant in our efforts to counter the inertia of "the system." We considered ourselves part of a small but noble American tradition, the "muckrakers," whom the dictionary defines as those who "seek out and publicize misconduct by prominent people." Though I don't recall specific conversations on the topic, I think our aim was to discredit members of "the establishment," "the power structure," "them." Perhaps we hoped that the citizenry would become incensed at their behavior, and would rise up and "throw off the yoke of oppression," or something to that effect.

At the beginning, we only came in contact with other like-minded folks who contributed modest amounts of money or equipment to support us in our task. We were happy to receive the gift of a Freiden Justowriter, a machine with a keyboard that spit out a long tape with holes punched in a particular pattern; you then fed that tape into a companion machine that in turn produced a column of text with straight left and right margins. We acquired some light tables, under-lit glass surfaces on which we mounted translucent broadsheet pages. We then pasted the columns of text, as well as pictures and other graphics on these sheets, arranged with headlines created on some other device, proofed everything, and then sent them off to the printers. (This was, obviously, before the advent of the personal computer.) We bought or were given some used newspaper-vending machines, and for a while we made regular runs to fill these machines and collect the coins. We hawked the papers on prominent street corners, and we mailed off some subscriptions.

San Diego in the late 1960s was probably as conservative a town as one could imagine, and its one monopoly newspaper, the *San Diego Tribune*, was clearly not interested in investigating potential corruption in city government. Opportunities for "muckraking" abounded. My dear friend Jan Diepersloot was generally regarded as the paper's editor, although we all filled whatever roles needed to be filled. In an interview in 1979, Jan was quoted as follows: "'We had key people in city government, in the IRS, and even in the FBI who helped us out,' says Jan Diepersloot, 51, the original editor and one of the paper's founders. These people would call and arrange clandestine meetings, real cloak-and-dagger things. We were the only opposition in town. The people that really knew what was going on were very frustrated…Sometimes the information [tipsters] gave us even exceeded our biggest paranoid fantasies."[29]

Soon we attracted the attention of people who considered themselves to be in the category we considered "them," and Newton's asymmetrical drama unfolded. It started with police accusing us of, and arresting us for, blocking sidewalks while hawking our papers. Some vending machines were smashed. One day some of us went to the office we had rented downtown and we found bullet holes in the glass door. There was another occasion on which someone had broken in and poured latex paint into one of our machines, thus permanently destroying it. I'm sure that the police were called on these occasions, and I'm equally sure nothing came of it.

The December 12, 1969 *Street Journal* reported that its new landlord had received death threats and had ordered the paper, the coffee-house, and the store to move elsewhere. The landlord, J. J. Olsher, was quoted as saying, "The extremists, the Nazis, are going to kill me," and "I'm not going to die for you people."

By that time we had rented a stately old mansion in what is now an upscale downtown neighborhood, thereby creating what would be my first and only commune experience. We moved the project into that house so there would be someone around at all times. We also rented the large house next door, so we had essentially occupied an entire block on that street. We had created some sort of self-styled "oppression-free zone" in which we lived and worked. As we inten-

---

[29] The San Diego Reader, *Notes from the Underground*, November 25, 1992, p. 20.

sified our efforts to report to the public what we saw as the truth, so the other side responded accordingly.

We hosted some public events with prominent left-wing speakers, including Angela Davis, a nationally prominent political activist from that period, and Dr. Herbert Marcuse, the outspoken Marxist professor of philosophy and politics at UC, San Diego. These events never failed to attract undercover police, who would look around for evidence of some sort of misdeed, on one occasion arresting someone for an illicit pill allegedly found in her dresser drawer. I have a distinct memory of Eldridge Cleaver, then a prominent member of the Black Panthers, standing in our kitchen and showing us the largest handgun I've ever seen (the times were full of drama, to say the least).

I recall that when it came to our attention that the properties were for sale, and a potential sale might bring an end to our lease, I had a telephone conversation about the situation with Mom and her husband, George. George expressed an interest in supporting what we were doing by purchasing the houses as an investment. We agreed that they would come down from Los Angeles in a few days to talk about it with everyone. The night they were in the house with us, someone threw a gasoline bomb through the open window of my old Volvo. One of our commune members was a US Navy firefighter, and I've never seen someone move that fast. He grabbed a large fire extinguisher, rushed outside, and had the fire out before the rest of us could comprehend what had happened. Beginning that night, and for seven months thereafter, someone was awake and armed twenty-four hours a day. I pulled my shifts, though from my current perspective I certainly question whether I would have been willing and/or able to undertake any forceful action had the occasion suggested it.

I recall that at some point we rented a piece of land with a small cabin out in the countryside to serve as a place of respite and refuge from the tensions of our activities in the city. Someone had planted a few small marijuana plants, but I'm sure no one could have identified them from the road. Apparently, one fellow (whom I don't remember ever being in the commune) decided it would be a great place to practice nudity, and he wound up getting arrested for that. I appointed myself to show up in the courtroom when he was arraigned, as a show of support, and I was arrested too, in this case for cultivation of marijuana. I believe I was placed in custody so as to prevent me from driving out to the "farm" and digging up the plants. Spending a weekend in San Diego County jail (before the charges were dropped) was an illuminating experience, one I intend never to repeat!

That was enough for me, though I never did sit down and think the whole thing through. I sold everything I had and moved to Colorado in the spring of 1970, met up with an old friend who had an extra acoustic guitar, and performed with him by a fireside that first night for five dollars. In retrospect, that period of time as a self-styled "revolutionary" serves me as an experiment in direct collective action to counter the ideals and methods of a dominant power structure. My experiences during this time left me increasingly unable to believe that action, even action emboldened by widespread agreement from peers and respected others can be infused with the power necessary to overcome perceived evil.

If in fact Newton's Third Law of Motion is the ultimate governor of politics, resistance to "what is" is ultimately doomed to failure. You can certainly snuff out objectionable behavior if you apply enough force. You can even overthrow an oppressive regime, as recent events in Egypt and Libya have shown. And if that's all you're trying to do, you can win. But if your real objective is to improve the quality of peoples' lives, to actually change the world for the better, the whack-a-mole principle seems to come into play. Whack 'em down over here, and they'll pop up over there. The characters may change, but the script will likely prove to be discouragingly similar.

I treasure those experiences at the commune with all those intelligent, creative people with whom I lived and worked and learned. That time was magical in many ways, not the least of which was the experience of allowing life to unfold, without the rational considering and making of choices about what to do, but rather with some unrecognized source of confidence that things would work out. That confidence and trust in events unfolding was to lead me to this day on my own version of the Magical Mystery Tour, what don Juan called the Path with Heart.

A FAMILY STORY—ON THE WRONG END OF POLITICS

My parents were classical musicians who moved to Hollywood in the early 1940s to work in the movie industry. I think they loved that work, principally because of the friendships they made and because they were able to play their instruments, at which they both excelled, and get paid for it. I've had moments like that myself. I've heard it said that if you hear a violin solo in a movie soundtrack from the 1940s or 1950s, it's probably Mom who was playing it. I recently received a small check for her work on Nat King Cole's version of "Autumn Leaves," which was featured in the 2011 film *My Life with Marilyn*. She also participated in several recording sessions with Frank Sinatra.

By the mid-1950s, the United States was focused politically on anti-communism. The Cold War was in full bloom. The effort to defeat the Axis Powers during World War II, principally Germany and Japan, had been organized around an abstraction called the "enemy." This way of organizing society was obviously nothing new in human history. That abstraction allowed the citizens of the Allied Powers to come together with common purpose and overcome most of the issues, beliefs, and feelings that might otherwise have divided them. With the war over, it felt natural to most people to transfer the organizing principle of "enemy," and by contrast, "the good guys," to the rivalry between former allies. With sides chosen, it felt equally natural for each side to fear and mistrust the other, as individuals and as political and economic systems.

On March 24, 1956, my parents received a copy of a letter from the Citizens' Committee to Preserve American Freedoms. It read, in part:

"Dear Friend:

"Thirty-five musicians have received subpoenas to appear before the House Committee on Un-American Activities on April 16th in Los Angeles. All have made contributions to the cultural life of the community. They include top-flight concert artists, members of the Los Angeles Philharmonic Orchestra, contract players with various studios, and free-lance musicians.

"The Un-American Committee has recently been reprimanded by the Supreme Court for conducting hearings in fields in which it cannot legislate. What possible legislation can they introduce in the field of music?

"Professional musicians in Los Angeles are engaged in serious internal problems within their union. The Committee's coming strangely enough, as in other 'Hearings' of this kind, is timed to coincide with this private labor difficulty. By the already familiar techniques of intimidation, it would seem that the Un-American Committee proposes to influence the course of events in this instance.

"If the past pattern of this Committee is allowed to continue, those musicians who claim their constitutional right to keep silent in the face of inquisition will be deprived of their livelihood and blacklisted from further employment. Already as the direct result of the issuance of these subpoenas several members of the Los Angeles Philharmonic Orchestra have been denied their right to travel with the Orchestra when it leaves on April 20 on the first of a series of goodwill-cultural exchange world tours. In this instance, therefore, we see not only the blacklisting of talented artists, but the additional injury that may well result to the cultural prestige of the United States in the eyes of the world."[30]

I dimly remember my parents trying to explain to my ten-year-old mind what was going on. I can only imagine how they must have felt. Both of them were called to testify before the committee, and they both appeared on April 19, 1956. They together issued a statement that

---

[30] A note to my excellent editor: I have reproduced this letter, and my parents' response, exactly as written, without reference to the Chicago Manual of Style.

read in part, "We would have been most happy to have discussed our views and activities freely with this Committee since there is nothing in our lives that we are, or need be, ashamed of. However our counsel advised that if we answered any questions about ourselves we must also answer questions about other people and if we refused to do so, we would be cited for contempt. He further explained that if we answered about ourselves we would have waived our Constitutional rights and would be forced legally to involve others. In all good conscience we could never allow ourselves to bring trouble to persons innocent of disloyalty in order to have the Committee consider us as fully cooperative. To hurt innocent people is to us inhuman, indecent and contrary to all the principles by which we have lived and functioned."

A further statement from Dad reads, "To the best of my recollection the following is, in essence, a true account of a telephone conversation between myself and [a representative of Universal Pictures, Dad's employer] held, to the best of my recollection, several days before my appearance before the hearings of the House Un-American Activities Committee. He informed me that a meeting had been held—presumably with certain officers representing Universal-International management. He said that a decision had been reached to the effect that if I cooperated fully with the Committee the Studio would be 'understanding' and 'forgiving', but that if I were not cooperative I would be dismissed."

When push came to shove, my mother responded to the committee by taking the Fifth Amendment, and then she simply went back to living her life. When her work in the movie studios came to an end, she joined the music faculty at USC, where she remained for the next fifty years. Her second husband, George, married to someone else at the time, mounted a well-thought-out attack on the committee in which he pointed out every contradiction inherent in its aims and methods. My father, in contrast, seems to have been caught in the middle.

According to the transcript of Dad's testimony, he was asked, "Have you been a member of the Musicians Branch of the Communist Party in Los Angeles at any time between 1945 and the present date?"

He answered, "I am not a member of the Communist Party."

The questioner followed up with, "Will you answer my question, please, sir?"

"Well, as I said, it is a compound question. Could you separate it?"

"No, it is not compound. I have asked you if you have been a member of the Communist Party at any time between 1945 and the present date?"

At that point, Dad said, "Sir, I decline to answer that question on the basis of the First and Fifth Amendments of the Constitution."

He was then asked whether he had participated in a plan to assist the Communist Party to get the Independent Progressive Party on the ballot in California. He declined to answer that question as well.

The transcript goes on (and on), recording committee members trying to get Dad to "help [them] understand how the Communist Party operated when you were a member of it, if you were." Dad is quoted as saying that "it seems inescapable to me that the only reason I am here is for the sole purpose of seeing that I am blacklisted, to make sure my talent and experience cannot be used to bring pleasure to the American people." He was angry, sad, and scared. Within a couple of weeks he was fired from Universal Studios, his contract there terminated because he had "brought disrepute upon the studio." The following February he and others filed suit against Universal Pictures for breach of contract. They prevailed in their suit, whereupon Universal and ultimately all the movie studios abolished orchestra contracts and hired contractors to provide the musicians needed for any given score.

I believe these experiences damaged his faith in his country and his culture, and in my mind it marked the beginning of his eight-year decline. Dad continued to work for a while under that system, for which he credited the only one of those contractors who was willing to hire him. After that he went into business with an acquaintance, but the business failed when the acquaintance withdrew. His death certificate from 1963 blames cancer, and I accepted that explanation for many years. I now believe he died of a broken heart.

CHAPTER 11

MY LIFE IN
THE MUSIC BUSINESS

During my first college year in Boston, I worked hard on my electric guitar. I listened endlessly to the guitar work on new records by the Beatles, the Beach Boys, the Astronauts (a great surf band from Boulder, Colorado, of all places) and the Byrds. Each time a new Beatles record was released, we were at the store right away to buy it. We'd bring it back to the fraternity house, and I would learn the chords. Then Michael and Barry and I would learn the harmony parts. I remember many joyful hours spent learning songs in between calculus classes and physics quizzes. Michael Rosenblum and Barry Schwartz remain to this day as close to me as brothers.

After my first year in college, I flew back to Los Angeles and drove with Mom to Aspen for the summer of 1964. This would be our eighth year there together, and we both looked forward to it. Almost as soon as we arrived in Aspen, I met the Hardy brothers, Gordon Jr. and Jack. Gordon Hardy Sr. was the dean of the Aspen Music School during the summer months, and dean of the Juilliard School in New York the rest of the year. Our parents got us together, and we hit it off right away. The Hardy brothers sang, Gordon Jr. (we called him Gody) played bass, Jack played rhythm guitar, and I played lead. We always seemed to find drummers around, so we had our own four-piece rock group. We learned a bunch of those same songs together, and even played a few gigs that summer. Many thanks are due to Don Fleisher, who owned and operated a little club in a basement on Galena Street in Aspen called Galena Street East.

The three of us continued to play when school began again in the fall, since Gody was in Cambridge at Harvard, and Jack was in college in Hartford, Connecticut. I recall many weekends that Gody and I piled ourselves and our gear (not much gear, in those days) into a convertible VW and drove to Connecticut to meet up with Jack and play fraternity parties, dances, and whatever else came up. Being a weekend musician also accomplished another objective, of which I was only dimly aware at the time, which was sidestepping the whole issue of trying to get a date, attend mixers, etcetera. That was never a very comfortable exercise for me; I think I just wasn't ready.

I believe it was the summer of 1966 when Gody drove back to LA with Mom and me, and somehow Mom scored four tickets for us to see the Beatles at Dodger Stadium. I don't remember the young ladies who went with us, and I don't remember much about the five hours or so we were at the stadium, but I do remember the twenty minutes the Beatles were on stage. We were near the front row, and the din coming from behind us was hard to believe. The Beatles themselves appear in my memory of that day as something less than overjoyed to be on that stage somewhere near second base. It's been said that the noise was so loud they couldn't hear themselves play, and I have no trouble believing that.

After the next year, our senior year, Gody married his girlfriend Annie and signed up for Officer's Candidate School in the US Navy. We said goodbye, and I went to San Diego to begin a summer job in the physics department, which I had been offered as part of enrolling in grad school. Sometime that summer I received a telegram stating that Gody had died in a car crash. The telegram was signed, "Jack." A few weeks later Annie came to visit. She told me that in fact Gody's death was self-inflicted, and that the family just couldn't yet cope with that reality. It was my first experience with a friend's suicide, but not the last.

When my time in San Diego was over, and after the drama at the commune had unfolded, it was Jack Hardy who said he had a gig in Aspen and two acoustic guitars, and I was welcome to join him. So in the spring of 1970 I sold everything I owned, my electric guitars and amps, left behind everything but a few clothes, and caught a ride to Colorado. I had no idea what might lay in store for me, but I was happy to be there, and playing music with Jack felt so much better than those last few months in San Diego.

That winter was for me the beginning of a truly magical time, for me and for folk, country, and rock music in Aspen. Many people remember the 1970s as one of the town's heydays; it certainly was that for me and for many of my musical friends. Live music was a treasure for the town, and of course I include the amazing classical artists and composers, for whom summers in Aspen were idyllic. The classical tradition continues, of course, to this day, but for us non-classical folks, working musicians for whom the Roaring Fork Valley is a near-sacred place, the music scene is now a shadow of what it once was.

Jack Hardy became a songwriter of near-legendary stature, especially in Greenwich Village and in Europe, and even in 1970 he had already accumulated a respectable catalog of good songs. He decided he would record an album, so in November of that year we packed up and drove to New York, where he and I and two friends from the East Coast, Bill Walach and Dick Coleman, went into the studio and in two days came out with a vinyl record, the first I had the privilege of working on. The picture of me on the back cover shows a young man with unkempt hair and huge sideburns, a big smile and joy on my face. It was a happy time. Jack is gone now too. I miss those brothers very much. A third Hardy brother, Jeff, was on the top floor of one of the World Trade Center towers on September 11, 2001. It's more than most families ever have to deal with.

After our return from New York that November, Jack and I ended our gig early one night and went to the Hotel Jerome, where we listened to Jan and Vic Garrett, a country-folk duo from Loveland, Colorado, who had been drawn to Aspen just as I had. I enjoyed their music, and we began a friendship that has lasted and grown to this day. Shortly thereafter I met John Sommers, who if memory serves, had piloted submarine-chasing aircraft in the Vietnam War. He had come to Aspen for a vacation on his way to St. Louis for flight training with TWA. He was typical of many people I met in Aspen who came there for a vacation forty years ago and never left. Jan and Vic and John got together and played at the Blue Moose, and occasionally I came to sit in with them. At some point they got a gig at the Hitching Post in Cheyenne, Wyoming, and I was invited to join them for a couple of weeks.

I remember renting horses with Jan and riding a little ways out onto the prairie. There was no sign of human presence, and I felt as if it could have been a hundred years before. One afternoon we all walked along the railroad tracks, feeling an Old West spirit, and a nondescript car full of four beefy guys came roaring up. They piled out, wanting to know what we were doing there. They were protecting their tracks, I guess.

Back in Aspen, we got some gigs together, and at some point we named the band Liberty, after an old fiddle tune. One day we were down in the Blue Moose rehearsing. I went up the stairs to the street, and there was John Denver. We had met through mutual friends, and in Aspen in 1973, someone such as John could walk down the street unmolested by autograph seekers and others. John Sommers had written a song called "River of Love," and John Denver asked me who wrote that. When I told him, he went back downstairs with me, announced that he wanted to record it on his new album, and asked if we could be in New York in a few days. We were playing the Moose five nights a week, so we said we had Sunday and Monday off. If memory serves (and it may be off a bit…who knows), we flew to New York on Sunday, recorded the song on Monday, and were back at the Moose Tuesday night for the gig. The song later appeared on John's album called *Farewell Andromeda*. The dedication of that album reads, "*Farewell Andromeda* is for all of you from Werner and EST and me."

We were at the Blue Moose during Ruggerfest, when the Gentlemen of Aspen hosted an annual rugby tournament, and the bars and clubs tended to get fairly rowdy at night. When rugby players get irritated with one another, chairs and tables might fly. Jim Gibbons, who I believe had played football with the Detroit Lions, owned the Moose. I vividly remember him vaulting over the bar to quiet a small melee, just as we were frantically trying to get our instruments into their cases.

Liberty, in one form or another, worked with John Denver for the next three years. I remember being on the road with Liberty in a motel in North Platte, Nebraska, when the phone rang. It was John, saying he needed an opening act for a concert in Des Moines, Iowa. We consulted our busy band calendar and tried not to sound too anxious to accept. On the designated weekend we loaded up two Volkswagens (one bug named Werner and one wagon named Honky) and headed east from Aspen. There was no Interstate 70 then, so we headed up Loveland Pass on US 6 (a mere 11,990 feet up).

About a half mile short of the pass, the bug blew its engine. No cell phones or AAA cards were in evidence, so we pushed the bug up and over the pass with the wagon, and then we coasted the bug down to the parking lot at the Loveland Ski Area. Vic and I stuck out our thumbs and caught a ride with two doctors who'd been skiing and were late for their rounds at Denver General. It was a wild ride. Later that day I rode the Greyhound with the bass amp to Des Moines, while the others crammed into the wagon for the drive. The saving grace was that I got to the motel, and its pool, with time for a swim and a nap before the others arrived.

For the remainder of 1973, Liberty played many club dates in Aspen. We also played with John Denver at Purdue University in Indiana, and on a mini-tour of the Pacific Northwest in Portland, Eugene, and Seattle. At these shows with John, we would play our set, then John would come on, and at the end of his set we would join him for three or four songs. At this point in John's career he hadn't yet achieved the superstar status he would within a year or so; for the trip to Indiana, we flew commercial from Denver, and we rented cars for the sprint to the venue. The flight from Denver was late, and by the time we'd driven to Lafayette, there was no time for anything but setting up and a brief sound check. By the time we had played our set we were tired and needed some fresh air. So we let ourselves out of the stage door, which then shut behind us with an ominous "click." Oops... locked out! A mad dash around the building finally yielded an open door with a merciful corridor to backstage, just in time for our return to the stage.

In 1973, Jan and I became very interested in the spiritual journey being offered by Guru Maharaj-Ji. Jan was initiated into his knowledge and meditation in September. I no longer remember when my initiation was, but it was shortly after that. Both of us adopted his methods for achieving inner peace and understanding; I recall Jan being substantially more adamant than I was about having that practice be the central thread of life. Near the end of the year, John called and invited us out to Los Angeles to make a Liberty record and then feature us on a TV show, his first special. Vic and John Sommers and I were really excited, but Jan recalls coming face to face that December with what she saw as a deep conflict between her newly found spiritual practice with Guru Maharaj-Ji and what appeared to be our clear path to commercial success riding on Denver's coattails. She tells me she and John Denver went out to lunch, with John making a serious effort to help Jan avoid "freaking out"; Jan says he was wonderful and sweet, but he didn't really understand the nature of her conflict.

John Sommers made the drive out to LA by himself. When he arrived, we gathered in Mom's house in Laurel Canyon. Sommers had filled several pages of a legal pad with lyrics and notes for a song he'd written, and he was excited to play it for us and have the band learn it. Jan tells me she was convinced that it was the "dumbest thing she'd ever heard." The song was "Thank God I'm a Country Boy," and the rest is history, to say the least.

During the week of January 7, 1974, we taped a segment on John Denver's first TV special for ABC. Included on the show was Lily Tomlin, whom I remember being very friendly to us, as well as the comedian George Gobel and David Carridine, the star of the television show *Kung Fu*. Jan's memory of that show was being taken to makeup and wardrobe and feeling very uncomfortable about what she felt was a plan to make her into something she wasn't; she remembers in particular being offered a short denim skirt, probably appropriate for the 1970s in Hollywood but not for a hippy from the mountains of Colorado. In the aftermath of his unsuccessful attempt to change Jan's mind, Denver abandoned plans for a Liberty album, and our segment on the TV show turned into our participation in an instrumental jam with a fair number of other people. I'm sure it was a disappointment to most everyone involved, but I don't remember being particularly upset. It was already clear to me that all of these and other opportunities to come were a gift from the universe, whatever that meant, and everything would somehow work out just fine.

After that episode, John Denver invited John Sommers to join his band, and after returning to Aspen to fulfill some club dates that were already set up, Liberty was ready for a transformation. In July, right at the end of the original Liberty, we went to Silverton, Colorado, to play some dates at the San Juan Bar and Grill, and we shared some of those dates with another band from California called Lost in the Shuffle. The upshot was that the three of us joined with three of the guys from the other band, and out came the new Liberty. It now consisted of Jan, Vic, Kent Lewis, Jerry Fletcher, Dan Wheetman, and me. Dan went on to be musical director of a number of musical plays, at least one of which, *Ain't Nothin' but the Blues*, made it to Broadway. He and Jerry now play in Marley's Ghost, a musical group based in Seattle. In my opinion, Jerry Fletcher is an impossibly gifted musician. Marley's Ghost came to Carbondale a few years ago to play at Steve's Guitars, a very small venue; there was Jerry, in the back of a cramped little stage, playing drums with one hand and keyboards with the other. Kent Lewis developed into a gifted songwriter, a role in which he continues to excel.

For the remainder of 1974, we played many club dates in Aspen. During that time we learned lots of new songs and honed a stage show that we and our audiences enjoyed. All of us played multiple instruments, so there was lots of activity on stage, even a brief choreographed dance number featuring Jan and Jerry in the middle of one of the songs. We were having fun, and it showed. Near the end of the year, John Denver once again invited this new incarnation of Liberty to make a record. Once again we journeyed to Los Angeles, to RCA Studio B, also known as Mother-B.

As I recall, most of that record was recorded live. There were vocal overdubs, but the basic tracks, including solos, were performed exactly as we had done them live over and over. I have participated in a number of recording sessions much more recently, and I can say that for the most part the art of making musical recordings has changed so much it's practically a different art form. Production credit on the Liberty album went to John Denver, Milt Okun (John's producer), and Kris O'Connor, his road manager and constant companion. But in my memory John was rarely in the studio. Often Okun was asked, "What do you think, Milt?" His usual answer was "Very musical." Vic says he made many suggestions to try to get a better sound on a track, and Kris always gave him resistance. Essentially, we produced the album ourselves, with indispensible help from the salaried denizens of Studio B, Kent Tunks, Artie Torgersen, and Richard Simpson.

Vic remembers us making verbal agreements with one another, before going into the studio, not to use any of the then-current pop-recording techniques, such as vocal doubling, self-harmonizing, etcetera. We wanted to be able to perform our record onstage. The band was highly collaborative; we all took turns writing and fine-tuning set lists, and my notes from that time show many of them.

I do remember one incident during a session in which we recorded a wonderful song by Kent Lewis, "Song of Wyoming," which John Denver recorded on his next album. John came in, listened to the playback, and gave us a "talking to" about production values (meaning, no doubt, stuff he would have added). Anyway, we added background vocals, including lots of "oohs," and I think the result did in fact enhance the song.

In contrast, when we recorded a cover of "Sweet Papa, Hurry Home," a Jimmie Rodgers song from 1932, Jan wanted to experiment with her lead vocal. After we recorded the basic track, she put down three versions, and then we all took a lunch break. We returned to discover that the three vocals had been mixed together to produce a composite with self-harmony, which whoever was producing that song had decided would do just fine. This didn't please Jan at all; it was an interesting lesson in the alternative Golden Rule, which says, "He who has the gold makes the rules."

There are some wonderful moments on that record, as well as some moments that still make me wince after almost forty years. The record was one of two that came out on John's fledgling label, which he called Windsong. The other record on that label was recorded by our dear friends and Aspen cohorts, Starwood (named for the exclusive neighborhood where John's house was). Bernie Mysior, the wonderful bassist of that group, recalls that when they went into the studio, the methods were quite different. He remembers playing his bass part all alone with a click track, basically a machine-generated metronome that keeps perfect time. Everything else was subsequently layered on top of that. In some respects that was a harbinger of things to come in the industry.

After the recording sessions were complete, our band was fifteen thousand dollars in debt. I don't know if we actually sold enough records to pay off that debt.

Anyway, apparently John Denver was happy with the record and our new band, because he announced that he was going to do a six-week tour in the spring, and he wanted us to again be his opening act. Plans were made, dates were set, and we all assembled at the Denver airport on March 31, 1975. By now, John qualified as a superstar. Besides his band and ours, the production included an orchestra and large-screen projections of movies and stills. Travelling with us were section leaders (string players, horn players, etcetera, as well as a conductor), and a new orchestra had to be assembled and rehearsed in every city. Our good friend from Aspen, Alan Garber, a talented singer/guitarist in his own right, played all of John's guitar parts during these rehearsals, and he served as our road manager as well.

At the airport we boarded the *Starship*, a Boeing 720 that had been outfitted with a variety of seating arrangements, two bedrooms, and a buffet counter on which meals were served. It seems to me we were told that our use of this aircraft occurred in between stints carrying the Rolling Stones and Led Zeppelin. Elvis had recently used it as well. As we took our seats, John stood up in front and said, "Welcome to the road." Someone quipped, "Big-time road," which John acknowledged, and which certainly felt true to us, hippy kids from Aspen.

For the next six weeks, we played more than forty concerts in thirty cities, from the South up the eastern seaboard to New England, to Toronto and the Midwest, and finally to Phoenix, San Diego, and San Francisco, concluding at the Forum in Los Angeles. The friendships made and deepened on that journey will stay with me forever. John Denver was a prince in my experience. I enjoyed my time with him immensely. We shared stories together, and we even discussed philosophical and spiritual topics, and I'm sure he also took the time to relate personally to everyone else on that trip. I got to know members of his band, which consisted of my old friend John Sommers on fiddle, banjo, guitar, and mandolin, Steve Weisberg on pedal steel and guitar, Dick Kniss (the Peter, Paul, and Mary veteran) on string bass, Hal Blaine (the drummer on countless recording sessions) on percussion, and the late Herb Lovelle on drums. Lee Holdridge was the conductor and musical director. I don't remember the section leaders' names, but I remember them as well. It was truly a magical time. I would love to attend a reunion of all those great people, but of course John Denver is no longer with us.

The first day of the tour we flew from Denver to Mobile, Alabama. We got up in the morning and dressed for the show that night. We had a couple of hours until the bus left for the arena, however, and someone told us that about a mile away, there was a submarine/museum anchored at a wharf, and that sounded like a good way to pass the time. We walked that mile, toured the submarine, and walked back, whereupon we all needed another shower and change of clothes. I've never really been a great fan of humidity.

Our days consisted of catching a bus to the venue, doing a sound check, perhaps rehearsing, having a meal backstage, and generally having a good time together. Then we would do the show, sometimes two shows, catch the bus to the airport, board the *Starship* and fly to the next city. On the plane, food was served on the buffet counter. The seating was open, and there was plenty of room to walk around and visit.

At the end of the first week we arrived in Jacksonville, Florida, and John decided we needed some recreation, so he rented a fishing boat. It was a smooth ride in the harbor, but as soon as we ventured beyond the breakwater, I became seasick, and I spent the rest of the ride lying down on a handy cot. Hal Blaine was in the other cot, claiming only to be sleepy. At one lunch stop somewhere along the tour, there was a jukebox playing a string of hits from the 1960s. It seemed like every time a tune came on, Hal would say, "That's me" (on drums).

When we arrived at the hotel in Cleveland, the entryway contained a huge table with a large Bible on a stand at one end. It was open to the twenty-third Psalm, which John intoned while the rest of us stood in absolute silence. Then we were shown to our rooms. One had a large, perfectly round bed, another had mirrors on the walls and ceiling, and all were completely different. Mine had a bed that was at least fifteen feet wide. The contrast between the mood of the Bible reading and the bedrooms was rather striking.

Just before our trip across the border to Toronto, it was announced that a collection would be made of any and all illicit substances that might be in the possession of anyone on the tour. I believe the instruction was, "Anything you wouldn't feel comfortable going through customs with goes in this bag." They were to be driven to Ann Arbor, Michigan, where we would be reunited with them after our trip to Canada. The customs folks at the Toronto airport were thrilled to be searching John Denver's luggage. Fortunately, we all stood around and grinned, knowing nothing would be found.

As we boarded the bus to the concert hall in Washington, D.C., the driver seemed a bit unsure of where we were going. The venue was called the Capitol Center, but he drove us to the US Capitol instead. In Kansas City, we were driven to the wrong city—it turns out that

Kansas City, Missouri, and Kansas City, Kansas, are on opposite sides of the Missouri River. On a very late-night bus ride from Springfield, Massachusetts, to New Haven, Connecticut, John was not on the bus but was instead in a station wagon driven by Kris, which was the way they had toured for years (with a complete sound system in the back). As they passed the bus, John gave us a "moon" salute from the passenger seat. A few moments later, everybody who could get to a window on the right side of the bus returned the favor. This was indeed "big-time road," but without all the smashing of hotel rooms and similar escapades we've all read about as punctuation to rock tours. This one was mostly sheer joy.

By the time we got to Phoenix—no musical pun intended—we were worn out and road weary. Some friends had journeyed from Aspen to meet us. They took one look and said, "You guys look terrible!" John saw to it that we had three days in the sun at a resort in Scottsdale. He also threw in an afternoon at a go-cart track. Kent and I passed on that one, preferring the quiet poolside to the roar of engines and the thrill of competition. Photos indicate a good time was had by all.

Finally, on May 9, we arrived at the Forum in Los Angeles. We were given a tour of the cavernous facility, including the alcove near the dressing rooms where we were told Bob Dylan had thrown up before his first concert there. Vic recalls that after our first show, he and Kent decided to go out in back of the Forum to smoke a joint. They found an empty parking lot in back of the arena that had been roped off and that appeared empty. With their backs to the lot, they lit up and passed it around. Whereupon they heard a deep voice saying, "Do you smell marijuana? Couldn't be. Nobody would be stupid enough to smoke a joint behind the Forum." They turned around to watch two uniformed motorcycle policemen walking away. Thanking their lucky stars, as Vic puts it, they walked sheepishly back to the dressing room.

This was the 1970s, after all. While pot was not a major issue on the tour, and while its use was never overt, it certainly accompanied us on all our journeys, and that was true for virtually every musician I've ever met, save (I assume) the classical ones in my parents' circle. In fact, before the tour began, we had been warned that Jerry Weintraub, John's executive manager and agent who appeared on the tour from time to time, had acquired a deep distrust of all drugs during his years of managing Elvis Presley. We had been told to "be really, really careful around Weintraub, or you'll be on your way home in a heartbeat."

Here's an interesting quote from Wikipedia about Weintraub: "Before turning to films, Weintraub's largest entertainment success was as the personal manager of singer and actor John Denver, whom he signed in 1970. Denver and Weintraub's professional relationship ended acrimoniously. Denver would later write in his autobiography, *Take Me Home*, 'I'd bend my principles to support something he wanted of me. And of course every time you bend your principles—whether because you don't want to worry about it, or because you're afraid to stand up for fear of what you might lose—you sell your soul to the devil.'"[31]

Weintraub was the dominant figure in all of Liberty's—and Jan's in particular—discussions about our professional future. Vic remembers a flight on the *Starship* when Jan and he were summoned to a meeting in a private cabin at the front of the aircraft. Vic thinks the other people present were Weintraub, someone named Sal, who was said to have discovered and/or signed the Doors, and Norman Weiss, who brought the Beatles to the United States. The three of them were smoking cigars. Sal looked Jan in the eye and said, "So what is it you want to do?" They were prepared to single Jan out at this point and offer her a chance to become a star. She shot right back, "Realize God in this lifetime." Vic says the room got very quiet, and then they were dismissed.

Liberty was designed around a hometown crowd that knew us and our music. There were lots of instrument changes that allowed us to plan our set lists around the music's flow, but that resulted in a lot of dead time. Weintraub and other management folks had us reorganize our shows to create more music and less shuffling around onstage.

---

[31] http://en.wikipedia.org/wiki/Jerry_Weintraub

Weintraub was also a big believer in toughening up his "charges." So after the tour was over, he wanted us to stay on the road and acquire a lot more experience performing. To that end, he arranged for us to play a room at Harrah's at Lake Tahoe. We began that stint on November 6, and we performed there six days a week through November 23. We alternated in this club-like room with several other acts, including Kenny Rogers, who had about reached the end of his association with the First Edition and was preparing to launch his solo career. About a year later he had a big hit with the single "Lucille." He was generous with his time, and I remember a meeting with him in which he gave us some tips about the business. The musician and singer-songwriter Jim Stafford was also in that rotation.

That room at Harrah's turned out to be a good choice for Weintraub's toughening program. We played three shows each night. There was a clock mounted in the floor of the stage. The curtain would go up automatically at the appointed time, whether the act was ready or not. The idea was to be playing your first song as the curtain went up. The same happened at the end of the set; the curtain would go down, and you were supposed to be nearing the end of your final number. The only anecdote I remember from that gig was the night Dan Wheetman launched into his version of Hank Williams's "Kawliga the Wooden Indian" as the curtain rose. The character in the song is somewhat stereotypical, so when we noticed an older Native American in the audience who had supposedly just lost all his money, there was some discomfort onstage.

The next engagement Weintraub had us play was a Ramada Inn in Minneapolis at the end of January, 1976. Meanwhile, however, the comedian/actor/musician Steve Martin had come to hear us at a club in Aspen, along with Bill McEuen—the brother of John McEuen of the Nitty Gritty Dirt Band—who managed Steve and the Dirt Band. They decided that we would be a good opening act for Steve, and so in early January 1976, we joined Steve at the Boarding House in San Francisco for two weeks. The format of that show was the same as the shows with John Denver; we did a set, Steve did his comedy act, and then we came back out and played several bluegrass tunes together. His considerable musical proficiency is much better known these days, but I'm sure it surprised his fans back then.

One association was winding down, and another was gearing up. John Denver and his management folks had decided not to pursue their association with Liberty. For one thing, they couldn't figure out how to market us. We had two front people, Dan and Jan, and that was an uncommon configuration. Next, we played every kind of music from folk, bluegrass, and old-timey to jazz and country. Our hometown audiences found those changes of pace interesting and fun, but the powers that be…well, we didn't fit into any marketing plan they could think of. And then there was the resistance they sensed in us, resistance to contracts and packaging and studio production values (i.e., vocal doubling and all the rest).

Steve Martin and Bill McEuen, however, had a different point of view. The tone there was set, or at least expressed, by Steve's crazy antics on stage and the Nitty Gritty Dirt Band's happy-go-lucky group persona. Their careers were serious endeavors, of course, but their attitudes were not, and we fit right in. And the San Francisco Bay area, where most of our performances with Steve took place, seemed perfect for that brand of entertainment.

The first time I met Steve was at a party in Aspen. My memory of that occasion has him sitting in a corner by himself. The transformation that took place when he got on stage was remarkable to me; I'd never really seen someone go from reserved and shy to dancing around with his banjo strapped on and a hat made of balloon animals or an arrow through his head. He was very good to us, and the association with him was great fun. He came to trust us to be consistent onstage and to prepare his crowd with our music and a bit of our own zaniness.

One night, some management types, perhaps his or the club's, wanted to try out another band, called Free Beer, so we took the night off. While I remember them as being quite good, Steve let it be known that he was glad to have us back the next night. Another night, Steve took the night off and was replaced by Junior Walker, one of Motown's signature acts. With Junior's crowd in attendance, our opening act didn't work at all. And then Junior got involved in an altercation with a woman working behind the bar, and there was some talk of an arrest before things calmed down.

We had our commitment to the Ramada Inn in Minneapolis to fulfill, and on January 25 we boarded a flight for Minnesota. Vic and Al Garber, who by that time was travelling with us regularly, drove a truck with all the gear, and Al met us at the airport. I think that the next morning was the first of many days when we awoke to great volumes of snow blowing sideways. The Ramada became our home for the next three weeks; we slept, ate, and performed there, and it was a couple of weeks before we could go anywhere. After two weeks or so of eating every meal in the Ramada's restaurant, we were desperate. One morning we opened the curtains and decided that the pancake house about one hundred yards across the parking lot was worth the trek. So we bundled up and got about ten yards out the door before running back inside. We had lived in the Rocky Mountains for years, but Minneapolis in January was a whole different experience.

That was an interesting gig, though. The Inn was on the outskirts of the city, and much of our crowd consisted of people who would come there by bus, stay for a set, and then board the bus and head off to some other place for some other form of entertainment. This seemed to happen over and over. When the weather finally warmed ever so slightly, we ventured to a mall, and we saw our record displayed in the window for the first time. It was a shock...for an instant it felt as if we had been revealed or exposed.

After our three weeks in the wintry Midwest, we were favored with a much-needed trip to Southern California. Steve had a short stint at the Troubadour in Hollywood, and he wanted us to open for him. McEuen had an HBO camera crew on hand for taping a possible show, and he insisted that they film us as well. I believe it was noticed that our stage show didn't work that well on TV. I remember watching Dan Wheetman chewing gum, and that was remarked on as something that wouldn't be acceptable. I think we could have been coached to present ourselves to the camera in a manner that would work, but that opportunity was not forthcoming. On the bright side, after one of our sets the door to our dressing room opened, a man stuck his head in, and he said, "Great show, folks," and he was gone. As usual, Vic was the one with the presence of mind to recognize him and say, "That was Roger Miller!"

We returned to the Troubadour in LA with Steve for five days in July, followed by two more weeks at the Boarding House in San Francisco. Finally, we returned with him to California at the end of October 1976, playing one weekend at the Troubadour, two nights at the Golden Bear in Huntington Beach, one night at San Diego State University, and one at UC Berkeley. At that last show the comedian and actor Martin Mull joined us all onstage for some bluegrass. Mull is a great rhythm guitar player, and the eight-piece bluegrass band that was onstage at the end of Steve's show was very well received. Vic remembers Mull sitting down with us and showing us some "great chords" to incorporate into a song we were working up called "Avalon," which was written by Al Jolson and recorded by Bing Crosby and others.

In January 1977, it was back to Hollywood to appear on the *Merv Griffin Show*, which was taped on January 26. Someone had said that "Avalon" was a favorite of Merv's, and we picked that song for his show. It went really well, and as we exited the stage during the applause, he acknowledged each of us individually. When it was my turn, I remember looking into his eyes, which were as clear and peaceful as those of anyone I've ever met. I've rarely come in contact with someone who was so present and in the moment; at least that's my memory of that encounter. We followed up that show with a night with Steve at the Roxy in Hollywood and several nights with him back in Aspen at the Cabaret in February.

On March 6, at the Aspen Ice Garden, we performed at a benefit for some now-forgotten cause with the Nitty Gritty Dirt Band, Starwood, and many others. There was a delegation of ten Russians who were shown to their seats in the front row during our set; they looked like the stereotypical Russians of Cold War vintage, with long coats and fur hats. Their entry looked like it was staged, or part of an act. It turned out they were there (probably reluctantly) as part of an agreement between our two State Departments to arrange cultural exchanges. After our set, we went back to our dressing room, which we were sharing with our good friends from Aspen's "other" band, Starwood. The Nitty Gritty Dirt Band had another dressing room next door. Bill McEuen rushed in and said, "Jan, Vic, come with me!" He asked them, "How would you guys like to go to the Soviet Union?" They said, "Um, OK," at which point McEuen said, "I'll be right back."

It turned out that, in the process of hammering out this cultural-exchange agreement, the American ambassador to Moscow had insisted that the Russians accept a "pop" band. The symphony orchestras had been exchanged, the ballets and everybody else had made the trip, and now it was down to the pop band. The Russians, in an apparent effort to avoid this potential disruptive influence on the youth of Russia, had rejected every previous suggestion the Americans had made. The Doobie Brothers were rejected for obvious reasons; even Linda Ronstadt didn't make the cut. Now they were down to the Dirt Band, and the Russians couldn't seem to find any disqualifying factors. Finally, it came down to, "We are an equal society; we cannot accept any group that lacks a woman."

So McEuen said, "Wait right there," and went running back to our dressing room. He explained the situation to Jan, who agreed to go. Then he went back to the Russians and said, "We have a woman in the band." Vic went along to play bass on Jan's tunes and a few of the Dirt Band's. Jan says that while they were touring around the Soviet Union, she made contact with the one known Russian follower of Maharaj-Ji, who was practicing her meditation in deep secrecy but who showed up to meet Jan and compare experiences. Perhaps that was the most real exchange that took place.

CHAPTER 12

TRANSITION TO A LIFE IN TECH AND BEYOND

During the latter half of 1976 and into the following year, I gradually came to realize that my participation in Liberty was becoming increasingly stressful. The quality of my experience of the band had shifted from a joyful ride in an amusement park to a more serious endeavor. I don't think I ever thought of that wild, magical ride as a quest for success; for me, it was always about having fun, learning new songs, and watching audience members enjoy themselves as a result of what we were doing—in other words, it was mostly about self-expression. It's ironic that as management shifted from the serious Weintraub group to the more laidback McEuen people, things felt increasingly stressful for me. As I thought of it back then, playing the music in a manner more authentic to the original context of the songs somehow had become "important."

I felt increasing tension within the group, particularly with my dear friend Vic, and that was very uncomfortable. I felt that I was no longer accepted for the musician I actually was, but instead I was expected to become the musician that he pictured in his mind. It hadn't yet dawned on me that this painful conversation was mostly taking place in my own head, albeit with occasional talks with Vic and others about the bass playing that was more appropriate for the jazz tunes that were an increasingly important part of our repertoire. The most painful thing for me, however, was the loss of the sheer joy I had felt in the first four years of the band's existence.

It never really entered my mind that I could leave the band. My Aspen music experience of the 1970s was itself an organic experience for me; it always felt like an unsought gift whose only purpose was to give me an avenue in which to enjoy being alive and I always thought of myself as leading some sort of charmed life in having these wonderful opportunities fall into my lap. I thought I could just weather the gathering storms, keep practicing my instruments, and just keep going. But the stress wouldn't leave; it just insisted, with ever-increasing force, on being heard. I had blockages on stage, moments when the notes just wouldn't come out. There was a series of nights at the Boarding House in San Francisco when an up-tempo solo was due, and I just sat there, unable to play anything. From this point of looking back, it seems so clear that it was time to face the issues and resolve them, but back then I didn't know how to do that.

Back in Aspen one night after the last stint in San Francisco, someone called a band meeting, and Jerry took it upon himself to let me know I was fired. In that moment I felt only relief. There were still some dates booked that I agreed to do with the band, but for me it was like being released. On April 4, 1977, we taped an appearance on the *Tonight Show* hosted by Steve; on April 8, we played the Dorothy Chandler Pavilion in downtown LA with Steve and the Nitty Gritty Dirt Band. By May, I had left Aspen for Denver on what would be a five-year hiatus from the valley I love.

I moved into the basement of a house owned by a good friend from the Roaring Fork Valley named Cindy. She was living at the time with her boyfriend, Jimmie Dale Gilmore, currently a member of the Flatlanders from Lubbock, Texas. Joe Ely and Butch Hancock are also in that band. Upstairs in the attic were my dear friend Lucy and a woman named Christine, who later became my first wife. I got a job as a food runner in a Denver restaurant called Zach's; the waitress would take the order, and when it was ready I would run it out to the table and bus the table after the guests had left. Then at night I played little gigs with Jimmie, and soon with his friend David Halley, another talented singer/songwriter from Lubbock.

Apparently, Liberty had further disintegrated in the interim, because Dan Wheetman showed up, and the four of us began to play together. Jimmie got us a gig in Austin, Texas, and so on May 25, off we went, the four of us and our gear in my International Scout. On May 27, we played somewhere called the Split Rail; on May 28, we played the Kerrville Folk Festival with Joe Ely, and during the week of May 30, we played five afternoons outside at the Armadillo World Headquarters, one of Austin's most famous music spots in the 1970s.

Back in Denver, life settled into a pleasant routine of working at the restaurant and playing music on many evenings. In August we booked a couple of nights in Glenwood Springs, at the other end of the Roaring Fork Valley from Aspen. On August 16, 1977, I clearly remember coming out of the Hotel Colorado to see a newspaper headline announcing the death of Elvis Presley.

Christine and I got to know each other gradually, with no pressure. She was working at a natural-foods distribution company in Denver. We enjoyed spending time together, and I joined her on her rounds, driving around the Front Range of the Rockies, delivering food to grocery stores and restaurants in the smaller communities.

It wasn't too long, however, before I felt the stirring of my life calling me forward. The previous year a friend had shown me materials from his correspondence course in electrical engineering. I remembered that the school he had bought them from was called the Cleveland Institute of Electronics and that they specialized in self-study courses. Mom was, as always, there for me when I called to ask her if there was any money available for me to sign up. She divulged that yes, there was an account that she had maintained for me since my bar mitzvah in 1958, and she gave me access to it. When I completed that first lesson, I had the clear thought that I was being led to the next stage of my life by something far beyond my sense of myself. That was the beginning of a conscious commitment on my part to living a life in which I would allow myself to be drawn forward, rather than making plans based on whatever information was available to me.

While that was going on, Mom invited me to come back to Studio City while I was studying. I asked Christine if she wanted to go with me, and so we arrived there sometime in 1978. Both of us looked for jobs. Christine wanted fulltime work in the natural-food industry; I signed on with a temporary agency providing workers on a day-to-day basis. I thought that I would work on a part-time basis, and I could then continue with my studies. I didn't see myself as preparing for anything, and I would have had no idea what I might be preparing for. I simply knew that I enjoyed what I was learning and felt that I should make some money at the same time. My thinking about that changed one day when the temp agency called and said it had a full day of work for me helping another fellow unload a moving van. He was a big strong guy, and I was not. I had never done anything remotely like that job, and I lasted about an hour and a half, by which time I was exhausted. I remember very clearly how embarrassed I was by this event, and I felt deeply that I never wanted to have that experience again.

The two of us lived with Mom and her husband George for several months, but it wasn't comfortable. I know that Christine and Mom clashed over a number of issues, not the least of which was me and my approach to life. Specifically, she was concerned, and rightly so, about my efforts to live a spiritual life. I realize now that back then I was still caught up in an interpretation of spirituality that said one had to do it the "right" way; I felt I needed to practice the right meditation in the right manner. I had to adopt the right beliefs, eat the right food, and on and on. Christine was a vegetarian, as were many of our fellow followers of Maharaj-Ji, and I was concerned that if I wasn't, and if that lifestyle turned out to be the "right" way to live, I might miss the boat.

My efforts to be a vegetarian didn't work out well. I lost weight and was unable to maintain a healthy, serviceable body in that manner. It's not surprising to me now that I was unable to fulfill my commitment to that other fellow on my moving-van assignment. In the years following those experiences I gradually relinquished the idea that I had to do the "spiritual thing" correctly. The fear of missing out on the possibility of true enlightenment was very strong in me. It would be many years before I would understand that enlightenment is about lightening up!

After several months, Christine and I took a trip to Santa Barbara. During the one day we were there, we made plans to move. On a second trip a week or so later, we found a small apartment, and she resumed looking for a fulltime job. We agreed that I would look for part-time work to allow me to continue my studies. It took her a while to find a job, but I found an ad in the newspaper almost immediately that attracted my attention. It was at a company called Moseley Associates, which was looking for people to assemble electronic components for the broadcast industry. It was an obvious fit, since I was studying electrical engineering. I took a test soldering various components onto a circuit board, and I was hired. I had not prepared a resume, and I had not submitted any documents showing education level, previous work experience, and so on.

A few weeks later someone there discovered that I had attended MIT. They insisted I take a job higher up in the company, and the first one offered was in the testing department, which I soon led. By the end of my five-year stint at the company—and my five-year hiatus from the Roaring Fork Valley—I was the engineering manager for liaison with production. I wore a coat and tie to work (the only time I've ever done that), and I had my own parking space.

Early in 1983, Christine and our friend Lisa Walsky (now Lisa Case) took a trip to Basalt, which is about seventeen miles from Aspen, and when they returned, Christine informed me that they had found a house to buy. And there was that tug again. Christine had found a job in the natural-food industry in Santa Barbara, but after a couple of years, the job ended because of some downsizing program. Something was pulling Christine back to Colorado. She thought a lot about what that might have been; I don't know if she ever found out what it was.

I also felt pulled back to the Aspen area, and to whatever might await me there. By this time I had come to fully trust that tug, and so I gave my notice to Moseley Associates and agreed to buy the Basalt house sight unseen. The three of us were partners and housemates, until Christine and I bought Lisa out. I knew that my old friend Al Garber was in Aspen and had started a small software company, so I called him. He said he had a job for me…just no money to pay me with. He and his partner Harry Wilker were writing an entry-level bookkeeping program, and Al was negotiating to license it to a big company for distribution. When that deal was done, I would be paid for the time I had put in.

All of this did come to pass. The program, called *Back to Basics*, was licensed to Peachtree Software—although they later buried it in favor of their own program. I'm sure that was a bitter disappointment to Al and Harry. The program was written on an IBM PC in a language called Forth, and it could be fairly easily ported to any other platform for which a version of that language had been written. The program was eventually ported to the Atari, the Commodore 64, the PC Junior, the Macintosh, and the Lisa, among others. My job was to make the program crash so that Harry could fix it, and so I spent many hours working with all those machines. During the two years I worked with Al and Harry, I helped others with their computer problems. By the time the company had disbanded in 1985, I was finding enough work as a computer consultant that I was paying the bills.

I had also formed a new band with some wonderful musicians from the Aspen area, a list that eventually included Dan Forde, Steve Frischmann, Frankie Thrower, Gordon Wilder, Paul Hill, and Charla Holloway. The version with Dan was called Dan Forde and Hi Country Music, and the later versions were called the Colorado Midland Band, after one of the two local railroads, which had seen their heydays during Aspen's silver-mining boom. Once again, opportunities arose for performing in Colorado, Southern California, and Las Vegas that "defied the odds," though on a smaller scale. I had the opportunity to spend many weeks playing in Las Vegas, most notably at Caesar's Palace, where Frankie's sister was married to someone in that resort's management.

There were wonderful moments with that band as well. One afternoon we were performing at a restaurant at the base of one of Aspen's ski mountains, and a gentleman was sitting at a table with his family. It turned out that he owned a huge ranch near Scott's Bluff, Nebraska, and he wanted to hire us to play there for a big party he was throwing for his friends. Once again, on the appointed day we flew from Aspen to Denver, somehow managing to get all of our equipment onto the plane. Once in Denver, however, the plane this man had chartered to bring people to Scott's Bluff didn't have enough room for all of us and our gear, so he directed us to go to the executive terminal and have some breakfast, and he'd get back to us.

As we nursed our coffee after eating, two young men in smartly pressed and starched uniforms walked up and said, "Gentlemen, your aircraft is ready." Thereupon, we grabbed our instruments and followed him to the door. Spread before us was a red carpet leading about twenty yards to the open door of a sleek, gleaming Learjet. This reduced us to giggles, and we clambered aboard, bent double at the waist to avoid hitting our heads on that very low ceiling. When the jet took off, we were jammed back in our seats as I never have experienced before or since. I assume that's standard procedure for a Learjet, or perhaps it was part of an "impress the band" program.

On a subsequent weekend this fellow's daughters planned an anniversary celebration at their home in New Jersey, and we were the surprise entertainment. We were flown there, of course; I no longer recall how we got all the equipment for a six-piece band there and back for one night, but I'm sure strings were pulled somewhere. It was all great fun. This group was not subject to the same stresses associated with Liberty's encounter with high-powered management and questions about "our future"; nonetheless, the band broke up, ostensibly as the result of some internal personality struggles.

A lovely woman named Kathie, whom I had met in 1972, came back into my life after Christine's passing, and not long after that she became pregnant. For me, the Colorado Midland Band's demise began when our son Luke was born in January, 1988. It became increasingly uncomfortable to be on the road for long periods of time, leaving Kathie to manage the household and a newborn by herself. I know that the story of the man who hits the road for work and leaves the woman with the baby is a time-honored one, but after six months it became untenable for me.

The way most people would probably tell that story is that circumstances intervened and caused me to end my time as a professional musician, but the way I tell it, the time had come for me to begin a new chapter. That may seem like a trivial distinction, but for me it makes all the difference. The first story makes me a victim of circumstances, and that story implies that the situation had the power to change my plans. The second story puts the power back where it belongs, in one man's journey through life, in his allowing himself to be drawn to new forms of expression. This latter story just feels better; that's the bottom line. What was to come, it turned out, was an expanded sense of being, happiness, and satisfaction, but it required me to let go of what was to be able to embrace what was to come.

Being a road musician was predominantly fun. Being a father, a technical consultant, a public servant, and a part-time musician has expanded my sense of what it is to be a human being. But that same sense of being effortlessly drawn or called forward to the next phase and the next phase after that continues to be the central thread to the story. Waiting for me back in Colorado was my family, my wife and my son. Also waiting for me was a community in which I have always felt valued. I worked again as a technical consultant, and when the local community college set up a Macintosh lab, I was invited to manage that process, and I taught there for about a year.

ABOUT POSSIBILITY IN POLITICS

During that year I also paid attention to local politics. One day, a town elder approached me to run for mayor. She said the town needed me, and my first thoughts upon hearing that were a combination of false modesty (it really *was* a boost to the ego) and wondering if I could really contribute something to the town in which I felt at home. As

I observed a number of meetings at town hall, I saw up close the dysfunction that seems to pervade American politics. I remembered Werner Erhard's analysis of the abstraction known as "listening." He used that word as a noun, and he pointed out that what passes for listening in our time is predominantly an exercise in comparing what we hear from other people to our own ideas and dividing people accordingly into "us" and "them," as I described earlier.

This observation prompted two questions for me. The first was, "Why has our political culture devolved from 'We pledge to each other our lives, our fortunes, and our sacred honor'" into a competition among debaters resulting in winners and losers, in which the winners exercise their sanctioned power over the losers, and the losers withdraw to lick their wounds and plot the overthrow of the winners?" And the second question was, "Is there another possibility, or can another possibility be brought into being?"

After a good deal of thought, I decided to run for office based on the premise that if elected, I would inquire into the second question, the one about whether a new possibility for political discussion could be brought into being. The population of Basalt was about eleven hundred people, and this seemed a perfect laboratory for that inquiry. During the campaign, there were a number of public forums for the candidates, and we were often asked what our ideas were about solving some of the problems facing the town. I doggedly stuck to my story. I was not running because I had answers to these questions, but rather I was running because I wanted to change the nature of the discussion. I described that change as a transition from listening to one another for the reflection of our own ideas to listening to one another as if the next idea proposed could be the one that makes all the difference, the breakthrough idea that would transform the range of possibilities. I believe Werner called this "listening for possibility," and I will use that phrase here.

In retrospect all of this sounds rather pretentious, but of the 212 people who voted, I received four more votes than my opponent and was duly elected. I considered myself in possession of a mandate to inject the language of possibility into our political process, and for the next four years I did just that. During the many meetings over which I presided, I continued to preface many discussions with a short speech about these different kinds of listening. In my thoughts, I continually reminded myself that the purpose of the experiment was to see if it was possible to alter the quality of the discussion and thus achieve better outcomes.

I will describe one meeting that will illustrate and exemplify my experience of those four years. A local businessman and former mayor of a nearby town felt that our town needed a public swimming pool. He took it upon himself to raise the money, so our board of trustees didn't have to be involved in that effort. However, it was up to us to decide where the pool should actually be built. We held a number of public hearings on the topic, and not surprisingly the choice developed into a controversy. One evening during the thick of the process we had an absolutely full house for the discussion, and all points of view were invited. I gave my usual speech about the nature of listening. As was commonly the case, the proposition that a better outcome might be achieved by listening for possibility was at least tacitly accepted without objection.

Many people spoke at that meeting, and one woman whom I called on expressed herself clearly and forcefully, though I don't remember what point of view she took. When she finished, I felt tension in the room, as though people with an opposite point of view felt attacked. I looked around the room and reminded everyone, "It's just a point of view," whereupon the woman said equally forcefully, "No, it's not! It's the truth!" Everybody in the room sat there in silence, and then a lot more hands went up. I was immediately struck by the definitive metaphor with which I think about that four-year experiment. In that image, I'm holding elevator doors open with all the strength in my fingertips, and when I let go, the doors slam shut.

By the end of my term, it was clear to me that what I call "adversarial politics" is one of those unexamined abstractions I spoke about earlier; it is fundamental to our culture that public decisions are a contest among representatives of the various points of view. The same process takes place, of course, in an American court of law. There is a great deal of talk in our political process, both local and national, about seeking and achieving consensus. In watching the political debates of the last few years, I have come to suspect that most of that talk is motivated by politicians wanting to look good and wanting to impress voters, who know deep down that to effectively address our problems we really do need to work together. But I suspect the politicians don't really mean it.

WHY IS POLITICS SO CONTENTIOUS?

That experience in traditional politics got me thinking about why our politics is that way. A few months into my term I worked with a consultant on such matters, and he handed me a small book written by Daniel Kemmis, a former mayor of Missoula, Montana, who is known as in some circles as a visionary. The book was *Community and the Politics of Place*, and while it's not his central theme, he discusses the nature of the political process that got written into the Constitution, and how it came to be that way. He describes an ongoing long-distance argument between Thomas Jefferson and James Madison. At the time, Madison was heading up the Constitution–writing effort, and Jefferson was "stuck" in Paris as ambassador to France.

As I understand it, the American Constitution was written at a time when deep divisions between debtor farmers and city creditors had already erupted into violence during Shay's Rebellion of 1786–1787. As Kemmis puts it, "The question came down to whether democratic citizens should be expected to work out the solution to such struggles directly among themselves or whether it is possible to adopt a machinery of government which would pump out solutions without requiring such direct citizen engagement." Jefferson argued long and forcefully for the former. He wanted to "educate and inform the whole mass of the people. Enable them to see that it is their interest to preserve peace and order, and they will preserve them."[32]

---

[32] Daniel Kemmis, *Community and the Politics of Place*, p. 11.

147

Kemmis goes on to say that Jefferson "had in mind a kind of civic or truly 'public' education almost totally beyond our experience." He explains the origin of the word "public," because that word was central to the Madison-Jefferson debates. I think this explanation is important because, as Kemmis points out, the word has lost most of its meaning. In Latin, the word means, "of the people." Kemmis wrote, "People in their separated individuality never become public. They only do that by a deliberate act of constituting themselves as 'the people.'" In Jefferson's eyes, the mere fact you have a lot of people living within a geographically defined area doesn't mean you have a public. Those people first have to declare themselves a community with shared interests and practices to have a public. I hear in Kemmis's words the echo of our earlier discussion about what it is to declare a new possibility.

Kemmis explains that "the great, hidden debate behind the Constitution was not about how to balance the interests of slave and free states, or of large and small states, but about the role of virtue, and of vice, as elements of citizenship. In the end, what emerged from the City of Brotherly Love was a view of human nature so gloomy that [only] the cynical…could have embraced it wholeheartedly. Thomas Jefferson, on the other hand, could never be reconciled to it." In Madison's *Federalist Papers*, written with Alexander Hamilton and John Jay, we find the opinion that "the latent causes of faction are…sown in the nature of man….The inference to which we are brought is, that the causes of faction cannot be removed, and that relief is only to be sought in the means of controlling its effects."[33] In the light of our discussion about causal abstractions, I wonder whether these words, which were enshrined in the Constitution, were mere prescience or self-fulfilling prophecy.

So the abstract notion of adversarial politics has been woven into the fabric of our culture since the beginning of the republic. But is that a historical accident? Or does that abstraction rest on top of other, deeper ones? What foundation is required to support the kind of

---

[33] Daniel Kemmis, *Community and the Politics of Place*, p. 13.

148

struggle I'm describing? Well, to sustain an adversarial relationship, you need to have separate individuals who happen to have differing points of view. But that's not enough. You also need those individuals to be attached to their points of view, to have "skin in the game." In other words, to have an adversarial relationship, you need people who feel the need to be right about their points of view. If you have two of these folks, but only one of them is attached to his point of view, an adversarial relationship will not be sustained. I've seen demonstrations by people who are versed in martial arts who demonstrate that principle graphically, by showing that if a blow is not opposed (i.e., if it meets with no resistance), it loses its energy.

Earlier in this work I noted that we get to be right, and all we have to sacrifice for that rightness is any power to change our experience to something more desirable. I mentioned that in the context of my explanation of the vicious circle that Werner Erhard described and its application to my experience of politics in the streets of San Diego. The same principle showed up again in my foray into electoral politics. Now, given that I am an element common to both contexts, I have to confront the potentially embarrassing question, "Is it American politics or is it me?" I acknowledge that the jury is still out on that one. My experiment at Town Hall in Basalt resulted in my conclusion that politics just is that way. I wonder if the lesson from quantum mechanics—that an experiment is meaningless unless it takes into account the observer—would apply here. I suspect it does. And if that's the case, then my mayoral experiment may not have been the most powerful experiment it could have been. Perhaps what was missing on my part was a sufficiently powerful context or existential declaration. I will leave that experiment for another day or for another student of the subject.

CHAPTER 13

LIVING INTO A DESCRIPTION

In this book I am suggesting the consideration of a new explanation for the world we see when we open our eyes in the morning. As I've said, we already have an explanation for this world that appears in our experience every day. The new explanation, however, is different in one critical respect. That critical distinction is that the new explanation, the one I'll henceforth call "the seer's explanation," says that the world that we see is actually a description of the world, rather than the world itself. Another way of looking at this distinction is to say that in terms of the existing explanation, the context for, or the container of, everything that we experience is space, or spacetime in Einstein's formulation. In the seer's explanation, this context shifts from the world to us, from spacetime to consciousness, from external to "within."

In this chapter we will look at a wide variety of aspects of daily life from the point of view of this new explanation. It turns out that when you look at life from a different point of view, everything looks different. The seer's explanation is about as different from the explanation we were given as young people as you can get. So it should come as no surprise that when you stand on the seer's explanation and look out at your life, everything you think you know about how life is supposed to work comes into question.

When we were little, our parents and others continually described the world as they were teaching us language and other standard practices. As we grew, we took over the task, incessantly describing the world to ourselves and each other. At the same time, our awareness became dominated by language, and language is very important to us because it enables us to get what we want and need quicker and more easily.

The purpose of having a description of the world is to provide ourselves with a set of symbols whose meaning we have all agreed upon, so that we can interact with each other. Imagine yourself, upon awakening in the morning, confronted with a stereoscopic visual image of areas of different color and shading but without the identification of those different areas as objects, and you'll get an idea of why we need a description of the world. The description is like an overlay, much as a bunch of lines and words—boundaries and labels—superimposed on a satellite photo of the Earth turns the photo into a map.

How do we get from that description we learned as children to our current situation, wherein we are confronted by a world that says to most of us, "Take me or leave me?" We get there by forgetting that the description is something we learned, and by forgetting that it is in effect superimposed over our perception of sensory information in the same way that boundaries are superimposed over topological information to create a map.

We are taught that who we are is contained or circumscribed by the outer boundaries of our bodies. Constantly repeating this story to ourselves reinforces our identification with our bodies, so that everything outside those boundaries becomes something else and not us. We are taught meaning (i.e., that actions and appearances have meaning to others, and therefore they should have meaning to us). We learn right and wrong, good and bad, naughty and nice, and so on, and as we master those distinctions we become more and more adept at getting what we want by pleasing those around us, and that behavior is constantly reinforced because it feels better to be pleasing others than not.

So our misidentification of the description of the world with the world itself becomes an explanation for what we see, and we all mistake the description of the world for the world itself. Werner Erhard had a wonderful metaphor for this confusion. He spoke about the difference between a menu and a meal. I visualize a menu that has mouth-watering photographs of the various dishes. He said (actually, thundered from the stage), "You mistake the menu for the meal! You eat the menu!" I venture to say that most of us human beings, to one degree or another, find life unsatisfying, especially in contrast with what we believe it could be. And so we cast about for things and people to fill the void, to make us happy, to give us satisfaction. But if we're mistaking the menu for the meal, we won't ever feel satisfied.

By way of contrast with the seer's explanation, the explanation for the world that we're born into says that the world is exactly the way it looks to us. And it says that the world is "out there," outside the bodies that contain or circumscribe who we are. When we live, when we express ourselves, we express out into the world; we perform our actions out in the world. I suggest that we know what happens when you have billions of people living into a description of the world as if it is the "real world." We see what happens when nearly everybody is emotionally committed to the description, so that they can be right about it. What you get is what you see when you turn on the news: scarcity, inevitability, intractability, and so on.

My interpretation of that, which isn't necessarily The Truth and which I offer only as a possibility, is that you have billions of people who know deep down that while they depend on the manipulation of conditions and circumstances for their happiness, they can't control those conditions and circumstances, and therefore they feel powerless to affect the quality of their lives. That feeling of powerlessness leaves us with what remains when we lose our power and that is, essentially, faking it.

But consider what happens if you live into a different understanding of the world, one in which the world itself is understood to be mysterious and unfathomable (in don Juan's words) and is separated from us by the explanation with which we interpret it. Instead of living into the world, we live into the description of the world. What does it mean to live into a description? The seer's explanation says that a human being is a focuser of energy; we *are* energy, and we direct our energy with the focus of our attention. Whatever we focus upon receives that energy and begins to grow, to expand, and to be amplified into the rich texture of personal experience. But we don't just direct that attention by selecting phenomena randomly; we use a description, an interpretation, as a way of focusing.

Mostly what we do is focus our attention on what we would like to improve or fix about our lives and the world in general, because in our common interpretation of our lives, and the world, there are huge problems that need to be fixed. Sometimes, if we're feeling good, we focus on what is beautiful and good in our experience, but in either case we say we're focusing our attention on the world. If you say you're directing your attention toward the world, and the world is a description, you're living into the description that passes for the world.

When a human being lives life from the explanation we inherit from our culture, everything is an "is." Life *is* hard, death *is* sad, taxes *are* a burden, suffering *is* unavoidable, etc. It should be noted, of course, that for some people, life is easy, death can be avoided for a long time, taxes can also be avoided, and suffering is mostly what other people do. But what about if a human being lives life using an explanation such as the one I have proposed? First of all, if you're living into a description, and you know it's only a description, you can experiment with changing the description. As you experiment with this new degree of freedom, you may find that you're not stuck with the world being an "is." You may find that the sheer dead weight of inevitability and intractability lessens and lightens your load. In terms of my map vs. topography metaphor, many times during my lifetime the boundaries of various countries have been redrawn and the countries renamed. We're not stuck with, say, 1945 boundaries, as we would be if we didn't realize that the boundaries and names form an overlay on top of the natural topography.

Most important to anyone who wants to live a joyful life, you can carefully choose or tweak the description you live into so that you are continually empowered to be who you really are and to act accordingly. I can say with complete conviction and confidence that a human being who acts in accord with who he or she really is performs actions that have a unique power that is absent in a person who believes himself or herself to be a transient in a permanent world.

TESTING THE SEER'S EXPLANATION

I spoke earlier of the scientific method, the crowning achievement of rational thought. It says that if you want to understand some aspect of the world, you develop a theory of that aspect and then examine the theory to find testable predictions. To the degree that the predictions confirm the experiment, you feel entitled to increase your confidence that the theory is true or accurate. To the degree that the predictions are not borne out, however, you then have to modify the theory to account for these observations and try again.

I suggest that anyone who wants to test the theory that's the subject of this book—that what passes for the world is actually a description of the world—has only one domain in which to do the experiments, and that is one's own life. Actually, I'm suggesting that we've all been doing that experiment all along, for our entire lives in fact. We have accepted an explanation for the appearance of the world and our place in it, and sure enough every experiment we've ever performed in our daily lives has confirmed that explanation. The result of that lifelong experiment, if one is paying attention and realizes that one is in fact conducting an experiment, is that the Universe is reflexive (i.e., it reflects back to you your understanding or explanation of what you see). I'm only suggesting that we become deliberate about the experiment.

So here's the experiment, the deliberate and conscious test of the idea that the world we experience is actually a description: Adopt a different description and see if the world conforms to that new view.

First, however, a caveat: If you do that experiment honestly, I suggest you'll find at the outset that it's not as easy as it sounds. To me it's like considering a physical activity that you've been participating in for a long time. Most participants in physical activities (sports, musicianship, etc.) have developed bad habits (i.e., habits of action that produce less than optimal results). Changing those habits requires intense concentration and commitment, and those habits usually take some time to overcome.

Habits of thought and belief behave the same way. It's one thing to work with a coach and modify some aspect of physical action, such as a golf swing, so that the desired result is gradually produced. It's quite another to change your view of the world so that you actually see that you are looking at a learned and practiced description when you open your eyes in the morning. You have to do it little by little. What I've discovered, however, is that the Universe will help you out if you're actually *doing* the experiment, which as Werner often pointed out, is different from thinking about the experiment.

STALKING YOUR POWER, STALKING YOUR SELF

Don Juan spent a considerable amount of time with Carlos introducing him to the idea of stalking as a technique to change one's idea of the world. To do that, he took Carlos out into the desert, and he taught him how to hunt. He pointed out that to hunt effectively you have to observe the prey carefully; he showed Carlos how to anticipate the animal's movements and regulate his own so that his presence and actions wouldn't alarm the animal. That task required great concentration, which had the added benefit of helping Carlos turn down the volume of his internal dialog.

The point of that exercise in stalking, however, was not to teach Carlos how to feed himself in the desert. It was to introduce the idea of stalking as a methodology that can be applied to oneself—watching for clues, for evidence. In this story, don Juan was urging Carlos to view the world as a mysterious, unfathomable place where magical things can show up, things that we ordinarily don't notice because we already know what the world is and how it operates. That's the idea we need to honestly do the experiment I'm describing.

When I say that the Universe will help you out if you actually do the experiment, I mean that if you actually approach your daily life as an experiment to see if there are previously unnoticed indications that you have more power than you believed you have, you will find evidence that you do.

Esther Hicks, speaking as Abraham, has suggested several experiments one can perform in this regard. The one I like to cite is the following. We are urged to pick two people from our lives. One is "easy to love" (i.e., easy to accept exactly as she is). The other is "hard to love" (i.e., someone who really would have to change in some way before we can love or accept him). This initially counter-intuitive experiment consists of taking the person who's easy to love and making a list of all her negative attributes, and then taking the person who's hard to love and making a similar list of all his positive attributes. She says that if you do that experiment honestly, making a list of attributes you actually observe and not making it up and not faking it, you will find that these two people will gradually show up differently in your experience (i.e., more in accord with your lists).

Doing the experiment honestly also means you have to put aside what you already know about these people, and put aside what you already know about people in general, which is that they are the way they are, and that's the end of it. I'm pretty sure all of us know people who don't always show up in our experience the same way. Sometimes they are easy to get along with; sometimes they're not. What if your mood, your expectation of your own experience at any particular moment, has something to do with how people show up for you in that moment? To watch someone else begin to be a different person in your eyes—as a result of your willingness to look at people not as objects with fixed characteristics but as aspects of a reflexive Universe (i.e., one that reflects back to us our idea of the world)—is to begin to sense your own power.

So to "stalk" yourself is to make up your mind to trust yourself and the Universe. It's to watch for indications that the Universe hears you and will respond to what you want to the degree that you allow yourself to let go of the culturally mandated obligation to make things happen and get what you need by cleverness or contrivance. This is the experiment I'm suggesting: consider yourself the source of the entirety of your own experience, and gradually drop all the blame and victimhood, competition with others, the self-importance, the petty lying and bending of the truth, and all the other things we do to get an advantage and skew the odds toward ourselves. A real Being in command of the totality of the Self would have no need of those contrivances. Let the Universe show you who you really are.

THE SEARCH FOR AUTHENTICITY

My advice to anyone wishing to experience the seer's explanation is to search for your own authenticity. One of my lifelong habits has been to respond to others' tales of difficulty and hardship with expressions of sympathy and commiseration. The problem with those expressions on my part is that even though they may produce some temporary measure of good feeling in myself or the other person, they're not genuine. As a result, I don't feel good when I try to be sympathetic, when I *try* to "be there" for someone else in his or her time of difficulty.

Before I encountered the seer's explanation I thought there was something wrong with me that would explain why I wasn't very good at commiseration. I believe I've always known at a deep level that if I encounter difficulty, it's of my own making. I know I can always trace my problems to an inadequate or incomplete understanding of who I am and what is required for me to feel good about myself. In that sense, I know that my problems are a function of the story I tell about myself. And I have to conclude that's true of everyone else as well, no matter how daunting the challenges they, or I, face.

Each of us has a self-image to which we cling mightily. My self-image is that I am a kind and gentle person, warm and caring and considerate of all the people I encounter in my daily life. I like that self-image, and I'm happy to project it to everyone, old friends and new. The only problem is that it's a contrivance. It's part of who I learned to be to ensure that people would like me and include me so that I won't be alone. I think that by far the most difficult thing any human being could possibly do is to allow that self-image to crumble so that the real being can emerge. It's a terrifying prospect, giving up the mask that one has worn for so long and that we have fervently believed to be who we are. Who might we turn out to be?

THE RACKET

Werner Erhard called this mask—this contrivance we adopted as children in an attempt to avoid feeling dominated and insecure—a racket. My dictionary defines racket as "an illegal or dishonest money-making scheme, involving activities such as bribery, fraud, or intimidation." In Werner's usage, he stripped away unnecessary implications and would, I believe, have defined a racket as a dishonest scheme involving activities that are in essence fraudulent. That definition makes our masks, our public personas, sound pretty awful. And to confront our own lack of authenticity is enormously difficult for a human being. But it's also the doorway we have to pass through to discover who we really are.

Werner goes on to point out that every racket has both a payoff and a cost. The payoff of a racket is what one gets out of it. What I've gotten out of my racket is the feeling that I'm not alone, that people like me, and that they will include me in their circles of friendship. For me, the payoff of my racket has been consistently rewarding. I have always had friends who welcome me with open arms. I have had a number of wonderful relationships with women, and two fulfilling marriages to two very special people.

When I got to college I was welcomed into a real fraternity, a group of men with whom I felt part of a group, an experience of belonging that was larger than being with a bunch of individuals. I've been to reunions of that fraternity, and I feel great joy in being with those guys, sharing stories of back then, and catching up on the intervening decades. I have a photograph of four of us on a cross-country trip after my graduation, in 1967, at Mt. Rushmore, posing in the parking lot with the four presidents in the background. I have another photo of the four of us from a reunion in 2011. The smiles on our faces in the latter picture are absolutely genuine.

When I left grad school, I found the community of political activists, and I loved living in the commune I've spoken about. I felt part of a group of people who were committed to the activities in which we were engaged. When I moved to Aspen, I found myself part of a community of musicians, many of whom I love dearly to this day. As I write these words in my favorite coffee shop in my small town, people whom I know come in and out, and the young ladies who serve me my favorite snacks and beverages are sweet and kind to this much older man.

So if this mask I've worn for so long is a racket, why in the world would I want to give it up? To be honest, I don't particularly *want* to give it up. It's just that I feel increasingly uncomfortable when I see my personality as a contrivance or as an act, which seems to happen increasingly often. And when people I love encounter difficult and painful circumstances, I feel increasingly inauthentic when I try to express my caring about their suffering in terms of how unfortunate they are, and of how circumstances beyond their control have victimized them. I simply can no longer forget hearing Werner say that the cost of one's racket is "only" love, health, happiness, and full self-expression.

As my inauthentic "caring" for people became more and more difficult to express, I often worried about what would replace it if I were to let it go. This is in a way excruciating. Do I not care about others? And if it turned out that I don't actually care about other people, would anyone still want to be with me? In that sometimes-painful self-reflection, a new distinction emerged. Within each of us is the limited being, the personality that we built for ourselves to survive. But there's the real Self within us all, the one that wanted to express into a stable time-space reality so much as to willingly forget real beingness and set out upon the journey of a lifetime with only feeling for guidance. That's the being I care about, and I care deeply about that being within everyone I encounter.

I find that it is useless to search for those who also have heard "whisperings," who somehow know, even if they can't articulate what they know, that they are more than they always thought they were, and that it is possible to lead happy, fulfilling lives no matter what the circumstances. I've been at this for a long time, and I will say with assurance that those people are rare. If you want to be with them, you can't just separate them out from the masses by looking for certain characteristics. Instead, they have come into my experience as a function of resonance, a shared vibrational frequency the Universe uses to put people and circumstances together. Because it is useless to search for those people, my racket is both useless and unnecessary with them. I have encountered a few of those people in my life, and I find that being with them makes the world real for me.

FALSE DISTINCTIONS

I think that one of the most interesting implications of the seer's explanation is that in its light the distinctions we use to divide people into "us" and "them" come sharply into focus. We use these distinctions to be right, to make others wrong, to dominate others, and to avoid domination ourselves. It's a powerful imperative that we learn from our culture, this effort to find ways in which we can feel superior, or at least not inferior, to other people. People accuse one another of not caring about others, of being self-centered, of having the wrong beliefs and ideas, of advocating government by the wrong principles, and on and on. I have, like everyone else, utilized these strategies. When I've used them, they actually do make me feel better, but only for a very short time. Justifying myself by making myself right and someone else wrong can bring temporary relief from oppressive feelings. I used that strategy with my mother a lot.

But as we've said before, these strategies don't do anything about feelings of powerlessness, because when you push against people you don't agree with, they tend to push back with a minimum of the same force you used in the first place, and ultimately nothing changes. In fact, from the view of the seer's explanation these distinctions aren't even real. Dividing people into "us" and "them" rests on top of the culturally derived assumption that there are all these other people out there with whom we are competing for resources, for friends, for love, and on and on. But the seer's explanation says the entire world, everything we experience, everything we see, is part of a description, and it's this description that contains the ideas of scarcity and competition. Competition for stuff, whether you're talking about money or love, requires scarcity as a predicate. If something isn't scarce, it's senseless to compete for it. When you see that, feeling the need for competition falls away, and with it feeling the need to do anything with all those other people except appreciate them for what they bring to the party.

Take just one example from the political debates: the conflict between believers in natural selection and those who insist on the validity of intelligent design. Essentially, the first camp believes that the appearance on Earth of life forms of ever-increasing complexity is a mechanical process, and the result of this process has been the consciousness necessary to comprehend that complexity. By contrast, the second group believes that consciousness or intelligence was the cause and not the effect of this process, and that the entire design, from one-celled organisms to humans, is the result of a supreme being, separate from and superior to us, whose unlimited intelligence was perforce equal to the task.

The scientific community rejects intelligent design as pseudo-science without empirical support or evidence. That criticism sometimes lumps intelligent design together with creationism, which holds that the entire natural history of the planet, including fossils and other evidence of the extinction of species, was put in place relatively recently. Elements of the religious community, on the other hand, seem to reject evolution as being driven solely by natural laws, which could not possibly account for the development of the organic sophistication supposedly required for intelligence. As Wikipedia has it, "some of the oldest and most common objections to evolution dispute whether evolution can truly account for all the apparent complexity and order in the natural world. It is argued that evolution is too unlikely or otherwise lacking to account for various aspects of life, and therefore that an intelligence, God, must at the very least be appealed to for those specific features."[34]

Aside from both sides trying to be right in their respective positions, and the infiltration of the dispute into the politics of so-called church-and-state issues, the crux of the argument is that evolution and intelligent design are mutually exclusive. As I see it, this mutual exclusivity in turn depends on the belief that the world exists independently of consciousness. Most scientists see evolution as a mechanical process driven by the laws of natural selection, and in that view consciousness and intelligence never enter into the explanation.

Viewed from the seer's explanation (and, I believe, quantum physics), however, there is no world apart from the description of the world, and to have a description of anything there has to be consciousness to create and perceive that description. The Universe (all-that-is) is just another way of referring to fully conscious, fully aware energy; it never stops creating, and it creates through ideas. Those ideas continually evolve to fuller and fuller expressions of being and of being-in-the-world. It is universal consciousness imagining possibility that drives the evolution of ideas and the manifestation of ideas into physical reality. Seen from that perspective, the conflict apparent in the default explanation simply disappears.

SPACE IS EXPANDING

To me, one of the most interesting of the modern physicist's topics of research and speculation is the apparently accelerating expansion of the universe. When Edwin Hubble first demonstrated in 1929 that the visible universe is expanding (i.e., that all visible galaxies are flying apart from one another), it was thought that, as a result of the Big Bang explosion, everything was flying apart into the static emptiness

---

[34] http://en.wikipedia.org/wiki/Intelligent_design

that was considered space. The controversy at the time was about whether the force of the original explosion was sufficient to overcome gravity and result in a universe that would expand indefinitely, or whether that mutual gravitational attraction would result in an eventual collapse, essentially the reverse of what we're now seeing.

However, current scientific thought is that space itself is expanding, creating new space as it goes. A common metaphor used to grasp the idea of expanding space is to consider the surface of a balloon. If you first draw dots on the balloon and then blow it up, each of the dots will move away from all the others. If you lived on one of these dots and viewed your two-dimensional surface-of-the-balloon world, it would appear that you were at the center of this world and all of space was expanding around you. This would not be due to any force between the dots, however, but would be due simply to the expansion of the space (the balloon) in which they are located.

Harder to explain, say the scientists, is the observation that the expansion of the universe is actually accelerating. Expansion can be viewed simply as inertia after the Big Bang explosion; acceleration in a physical sense, however, would seem to require some force pushing things apart. If you are convinced that the physical universe exists "out there," apart from any observers who might be present, and if you want to explain the physical universe, you have to account for that force. Physicists are now proposing what they call dark energy as the responsible agent, but its existence is hypothetical and its nature is a matter of speculation. Furthermore, according to a Wikipedia article, since by calculation it would be of very low concentration, it "is unlikely to be detectable in laboratory experiments."[35]

From the perspective of the seer's explanation, however, what we think of as the physical universe is actually a description, which we all accept, of something don Juan called utterly "mysterious and unfathomable." Descriptions don't have the same mechanical nature, the same immutability that a law-based world would have. You can

---

[35] http://en.wikipedia.org/wiki/Dark_energy

think about space—which is said to be expanding at an accelerating rate—as an idea, an abstraction that we use to contain and separate objects. (Similarly, you can think about time as an abstraction that we use to contain and separate events, but here we follow convention and just consider the expansion of spacetime.)

So space is said to contain objects, which are made of matter, but matter is more fundamentally energy. And now physicists say that spacetime is infused with energy. So when spacetime expands, it implies that the amount of energy in play (i.e., physically manifested) is increasing. And the acceleration of that spatial expansion reflects the apparent fact that the amount of energy involved in our time-space reality is increasing at an accelerating rate.

I find that when I make an effort to grasp these ideas, I continually run up against the culturally unexamined assumption that the context for all this is space itself. It seems to require a great degree of commitment and focus to shift that perspective to one in which the context is really consciousness or awareness, and that space, time, and spacetime are abstract ideas within that context. If space were the ultimate context for everything we perceive and think about, what could it mean to discover, as scientists have, that space is expanding, let alone expanding at an increasing rate? Wouldn't space then be expanding in some larger container or context? What could it be expanding into?

With some effort then, let's return to exploring these ideas using awareness as the context, which is what the seer's explanation calls for. What causes the amount of energy manifested in our time-space reality to increase? Well, there are currently some seven billion human energy sources around, at least those that we know about, and all of us are examining our world and our circumstances. If you take the perspective of your real Self—and doing that requires even more commitment and focus—you examine your circumstances and immediately know what you'd like better, more of, less of, or different from. Then you focus your attention on the new possibility you've created. Focusing your attention is like aiming a fire hose; focused attention directs energy to flow in the direction in which you're focused. That's the process by which more energy enters the time-space reality you inhabit. It enters the time-space reality from *you*.

In this view, each of us is the source of the energy made manifest in our world. And the observation that the volume of space is increasing at an accelerated rate, in this interpretation, tells us that all of us are together creating possibility at an increasing rate. The word that I think comes closest to expressing this idea is "synergy," which my dictionary defines as "the working together of two or more people, organizations, or things, especially when the result is greater than the sum of their individual effects or capabilities." When I consider the hopes and aspirations of all the people in our world, I find that this explanation works for me.

LOSING THE HUMAN FORM

I find a very interesting reference in Castaneda's books to the idea of losing the human form. Don Juan doesn't mention the topic directly; it enters the story (after his disappearance from Carlos's experience) through one of his other apprentices, a woman named Elena, also known as La Gorda (in reference to her physical size prior to her transformation under don Juan's tutelage). She claims that losing the human form gives her an advantage in freeing her from certain emotional and physical constraints on her aspiration of becoming a woman of knowledge. When it happens to Carlos, and Elena names it as such, he describes losing the human form as an experience in which he feels extraordinarily painful sensations progressing slowly from his head to his toes, a process taking place over about a two-hour span. Without don Juan around to provide an explanation or a way of considering the experience, I was, upon reading the story, left to wonder what it was all about, and more importantly whether it was somehow an essential component in his eventual recollection of heightened awareness, and of events and people whom he found no way of integrating into the usual linear chronology of his life.

The seer's explanation appears, however, to lead to a useful inquiry when considering this story. As I've said before, when we open our eyes and look at the world as an "is," we see ourselves and each other as physical objects in a context called the world. My physical identity, for example, appears to end at a boundary called my skin. Is that a real distinction, the distinction between myself and everything and everybody else? We take that distinction for granted, but does it hold up under scrutiny? Perhaps the strongest argument for that distinction, in an experiential sense, is that most of us have physical sensations and motor control as a result of stimulation of nerve endings throughout the volume of space occupied by our bodies and none beyond those boundaries.

But once again, the seer's explanation forces us to abandon the idea of space as the ultimate context and replace it with awareness. In our awareness, there is only "here" when considering location. No one has ever experienced "there." When you learn to view the world from this vantage point, the distinction called "out there" disappears. In my use of the word "seer" I refer to someone who knows that what we see when we look at the world is a description, and a seer knows that that description lives in a different domain from the world we are convinced is "out there." Again, you can think of the film projector for a visual reference. Clearly, the film and the "world" that is projected onto the screen have their existence in different domains, and we don't notice that difference if we become engrossed in the movie.

We mistake our description of the world for the world itself, and we use this description as an explanation of all the sensory input our bodies receive. The boundary between "me" and "not me" is an element of the explanation we use for the world we perceive. That explanation requires that you think of yourself as an object among objects, with all that implies. We will continue to inquire further into implications of considering ourselves objects among objects. For now, I will just suggest the possibility that the distinction we all make between "me" and "not me" is an artificial distinction. Ultimately then, this distinction would be a superstition.

Please notice that I'm not claiming that the statement, "the distinction between 'me' and 'not me' is an artificial distinction," is right or true. I'm saying it's not an issue of whether or not it's true. Asking if it is true amounts to asking if the seer's explanation is true, and I'm saying that asking if the seer's explanation is true is the wrong question. The better question is, "Does the seer's explanation give me more power to live a joyful life as a free being than the explanation that I am an object among objects?" What are the implications, and perhaps the usefulness, of losing the human form (i.e., abandoning the distinction that I am an object circumscribed by my skin)? That's what we will examine next.

CHAPTER 14:

LIVING THE SEER'S EXPLANATION

In this book I've essentially been arguing three propositions. The first is that the world we believe we are interacting with is in fact a description of the world rather than the world itself. The elements of this description are a collection of symbols we use to interpret, manage, and communicate about the sensory input to which we are constantly exposed. That range of symbols includes all the objects with which we're familiar, including our own bodies, as well as all the types of events we witness in which these objects can interact with one another.

By way of example, I cited earlier a particular collection of visual and tactile vibrational impressions that I interpret as a kitchen counter. I isolate that collection of impressions and sensations from the background, and the remainder of the impressions and sensations then becomes what could be thought of as not-kitchen-counter, or as the context in which the counter appears. The kitchen counter is one of the elements of a description, one that I use to keep other objects, other elements of my description, from falling on the floor, which is one of the many possible events that could take place within the terms of my description.

The second proposition I have argued is that the description we are focused on provides us with an explanation for the presence of the objects we encounter and the events we witness and, most significantly, for our apparent presence among them and our relationship to them. This explanation then serves as a recognizable, stable, and coherent platform within which we can explore the range of options of action that we can imagine and then select for ourselves a path among them, a path through life. Furthermore, we select this one possible world by filtering out all the others, much as a television allows us to select only one of the multitudes of programs available.

To illustrate this second proposition, consider that first I need a description of the objects within my field of view before I can consider what I can do with them. So I have isolated within my visual field a kitchen counter and a laptop, as well as the all-important coffee cup. Now I can consider locating the laptop on the counter so that it stays in one place and I can interact with it. And, I know that by performing a particular sequence of actions using my body and the laptop, I can generate and observe a pattern of dots appearing on the screen, which I can interpret as a representation of the ideas and thoughts I have. This last piece of the description serves as an example of what I would call operating my knowledge of the world.

Now I have an explanation for the presence of all the objects within my field of view and for my presence among them. I have assembled all these objects in relation to the one I call my body so that I can use the laptop to write this book, and I can use the coffee cup and its contents to sharpen my focus. I have of course left out myriad details in setting down this explanation. That leaving-out process is an example of the way I filter out all the symbols—and all my thoughts about those symbols—that aren't necessary to get these ideas onto the screen. Other examples of what got filtered out include all the other thoughts that weren't relevant and all the other objects that play no part in rendering my thoughts. And I exclude as well the entire range of vibrational information "out there" upon which I'm not focusing, such as all the frequencies of light that my eyes haven't evolved to perceive.

The third of my propositions goes as follows: The description I use to make sense of the world is the one I learned from the people with whom I interacted when I was young. As the use of this description became second nature to me, I mistook it for something external to me, something over which I had no control, something that constituted the context or arena in which I performed whatever actions I would perform. In other words, instead of living into the world, I actually learned to live into the description of the world I had adopted. And ultimately, by recognizing that I have mistaken the description of the world for the world itself, I now have a new explanation to live from, one in which *I am the context in which my world exists and not the other way around*. I call this new explanation the seer's explanation.

There are implications to living an explanation, or living from one, just as there are implications to making choices in any area of life. The power of consciously choosing an explanation is that it argues for an entire body of choices that differ considerably from the body of choices argued for by a substantially different explanation—and the seer's explanation is about as different from the cultural default as you can get. You can, of course, stick with an explanation of the world you already know, and then seek to change your experience or the quality of your life one choice at a time, but what you're really doing is rearranging the existing set of options into some other configuration.

Or you can adopt a different explanation and decide to live it, whereupon an entirely new set of choices appears. The difference between those approaches is the difference between just going through the motions, on the one hand, and living as if life is a daring adventure, on the other. Helen Keller said, "Life is either a daring adventure or nothing." In that light, choosing an explanation to live from means shifting the criterion by which you make the choice—from the explanation's truth to its ability to reconnect you with your natural power.

I will now examine a number of aspects of life from the point of view of the seer's explanation. I want to emphasize over and over that I believe it's useless to evaluate this explanation in the context of separating truth from fiction. I have, however, found during the course of my life that living *as if it were true* has brought me a sense of peace and self-acceptance I had not found in living from the "normal," culturally derived one.

MORE ABOUT LOSING THE HUMAN FORM

What are the implications of abandoning the human form (i.e., the belief that you are circumscribed by your skin), and instead considering everything within your field of view to be on the same footing? I suggest that if you examine that possibility honestly, either because you see the world that way or because you consciously make a decision to try out that explanation rather than just thinking about it, one of the first things that happens is that you begin to lose the feeling that you're living in a dangerous world. The idea of danger rests or sits on top of the belief that you are your body, and your body is an object among objects. If there are objects outside of you that can act upon you against your will, especially if some of those objects are active objects (i.e., conscious, willful objects like other people), then those objects can adversely affect you. By the way, I use the phrase "begin to lose the feeling" to indicate that this shift doesn't happen all at once; patience and steadfastness are required to gain this result.

Notice also that the belief that you are an object among objects is required by, and actually leads to, the feeling of being a victim. You can't be a victim when you are creating the entirety of the world you experience—except of course if you consider yourself to be a victim of your own beliefs. Victimhood requires the belief that you're an object among objects. But beyond that, observing the behavior of those other objects out there as they appear to affect you, coupled with the obvious fact that you can't control them, will eventually leave you with the feeling of being a victim of others or of circumstances, which in turn leaves you feeling powerless. Releasing the identification with your body causes that entire victimhood racket to crumble.

Now there's good news and bad news about that. The bad news is that the feeling of being a victim is a key component—for many, many people—of the strategy they have evolved for dealing with other people, particularly people in perceived positions of power. In other words, the feeling of being a victim is an essential part of almost everybody's racket. What's the payoff of that racket? The payoff is that I have someone or something to blame when I don't get what I want; it's much easier to go there than to recognize that I have a belief that's keeping me from feeling worthy of what I wanted. Changing beliefs nurtured for a lifetime is very hard work; feeling like a victim is much easier.

If you abandon the human form as I've described above, however, there are no objects outside of you. There are only possibilities, and possibilities only become actualized in your experience when you focus your attention on them. Fortunately for you, and for all of us, simply having a thought doesn't make it actualize in your experience. For something to actualize, a creative being has to feed it and give it what we can think of as a life of its own. I say fortunately because my mind often seems full of thoughts that I would never want to find their way into reality. Because thoughts don't actualize until they have been fed and nurtured, there is a lag between the thought and the manifestation that allows one to "get off it," or to change the subject or the tone of the thought.

That lag, however, turns out to be a challenge for someone stalking his or her own power. If you experience an unpleasant event in your life, and it occurs to you that there is a better way of looking at that event (i.e., an interpretation that allows you to sense your power), you may well not experience a sudden transformation that changes everything and gives you a powerful reinforcement of your re-interpretation. You have to practice the new interpretation, just as if you were seeking to change a bad habit into a good one. Because you have practiced the self-limiting interpretation for a long time, it takes time for the new habit of thought to become dominant enough to change the way that topic manifests in your life. One can get discouraged. The antidote to that difficulty is persistence. I can say from my own experience that eventually the desire for change will be strong enough that persistence becomes progressively easier.

There are also many techniques available for making this process a bit easier. I think that by far the most powerful class of such techniques is those that help to quiet the internal dialog. It is difficult even to notice that a particular event triggers a negative or self-limiting thought process if the overall volume of thought is too high. I notice that when I fail to consistently practice that calming of the mind, I spend large portions of my day failing even to notice the distinction between myself and the din of what I earlier called that hyperlinked mind. By far the most powerful tool I have at my disposal is the meditation I was taught back in 1973; as it happens, I've been practicing that technique for nearly forty years, as of this writing.

Don Juan introduced Carlos to another such technique, which he called, "the right way of walking." I have found that technique useful as well, so I cite it here. The right way of walking amounts to walking with your eyes not quite focused but paying attention to everything in your field of view. The effort to perform that task continuously leaves little energy for feeding the mind's excessive motion through its trains of thought. He also suggested curling the fingers as a way of increasing the amount of focus used on the technique, thus leaving even less for thinking.

When I first learned these and other techniques for quieting the mind, I made a common misinterpretation of their purpose and meaning. Like many others with whom I compared notes, I made the assumption that since withdrawing attention from the mind's activities was the goal, the mind must somehow be bad. I remember back then people speaking about "killing the mind." I have no doubt that these thoughts were seriously misguided. From my current perspective, they look like just one more attempt to be "right" or to live the "right way." That goes along with other "spiritually correct" practices such as eating the right foods, drinking (or not drinking) the right beverages, and most especially, believing the right things. That may be the greatest trap awaiting every unsuspecting seeker of truth: making that search right.

A SHORT PERSONAL STORY— RECONTEXTUALIZING MY MOTHER

I have spoken elsewhere in this book of my often-contentious relationship with my mother. For decades I blamed that contentiousness on her refusal to be open to my ideas, my discoveries, and my spiritual practices. Of course it was all her fault. I was just being the scientist that I am, allowing the experimental evidence of my inquiries to take me wherever they might lead. And because my seeking was "spiritually correct," I was entirely justified in my impatience with her and my resentment of her refusal to support my endeavors, both emotionally and financially. Couldn't she see how important my work was? Why was she being so old-fashioned, so stubborn, and so hard to deal with?

Of course, from my current perspective, I can only marvel at her patience, her tolerance, and her forbearance, which I sometimes think I would be hard-pressed to duplicate or even emulate. There are times now when I find myself wishing I had been more appreciative, more respectful, and a lot humbler. Because her resistance to my ideas (and behavior) seemed so unfair, I allowed my frustrations to build up year after year. Furthermore, because I considered frustration to be distinctly unspiritual, I didn't allow myself to experience the frustration and allow it to just be, and so it gradually built up into anger and resentment. In time I became a victim of my mother's dominating personality, having given up my power to determine the quality of my own life in favor of having someone to blame. All this brings to mind yet another of Werner Erhard's sayings: "In life, you either have the results you want or the reasons why not."

I say that there are *times* when I wish I had behaved more appropriately with my mother. As I said earlier, that's because I found after she physically left the world that I could view that entire aspect of our relationship in a completely different light. A couple of weeks after she passed I had a dream about her. In the dream she appeared to me as a little girl, dressed in a little white dress with a bow in her hair, much like she appears in an old photograph I have of her. As she walked across my field of view, she smiled at me and said she was off to school. I awoke from the dream with the distinct impression that she was letting me know she was off to meet with her spiritual guides, with whom she would consider the lifetime she had just lived and the lessons to be gained from it. And now the recontextualization of my mother is largely complete. I see her as having chosen to be here with me all these years, to serve as my life coach, the sort of coach who will not let you alone until you realize your potential.

POWER PLANTS

I would wager that for the vast majority of people in Western culture who seek a deeper understanding of the meaning and purpose of life, so-called power plants have been at least an occasional feature of the landscape, as they have been of mine. My first real girlfriend introduced me to marijuana after college graduation. So actually, she introduced me to pot and sex at about the same time. My first use of pot was on the patio of Mom's house in Los Angeles while Mom was in Aspen. Within moments I knew that the smoke would be a long-term companion; colors became more vibrant, the cool breeze became more refreshing, and so on. It was as if a fog had lifted, and everything became clearer.

I have left this issue alone until I had discussed the seer's explanation so that I could speak about it in the way I view it now, rather than the way I may have viewed it then. While I never encountered marijuana at MIT, by the time I became part of the antiwar community in San Diego it was ubiquitous, and it has remained a part of my experience ever since. While I did experiment in a very limited way with other substances, including LSD, "magic" mushrooms, peyote, and cocaine, I dropped them permanently from my experience several decades ago. From Castaneda's description of don Juan's "little smoke," which he said included the powerful substances Datura inoxia (jimson weed), Lophophora williamsii (peyote) and a hallucinogenic mushroom of the genus Psilocybe, my experiences were much gentler than his.[36]

I have retained the marijuana smoke as an aid, however, because if I use it carefully it continues to assist me in my journey by temporarily lifting the fog. I consider it an essential element of the seeker's toolkit in the same way that a person traversing an apparently limitless topographical expanse might climb a hill to get his or her bearings. I find it very useful in answering such questions as "Am I making progress?" or "Am I heading in the right direction?"

---

[36] Carlos Castaneda, *Journey to Ixtlan*, p. 7.

Marijuana has certainly been a friend to many generations of musicians, though likely not in the classical music circles in which I was raised. I joke sometimes with other long-time Aspen musicians about how one can get a bit of a buzz just by walking through one of the town's many alleys, particularly those that run behind any of the clubs or bars we used to perform in. It was also a key component of life in the commune; I clearly remember my companion on one of those middle-of-the-night patrols in the street watching over our friends in the house, saying, "Tomorrow when we get to work [on the newspaper], we can smoke a joint and get an idea." These were the words of a fellow, Lowell Bergman, who years later made a name for himself in investigative journalism as Mike Wallace's producer on *60 Minutes*. And marijuana could almost be listed in the acknowledgements of this present work, not only because I have used it occasionally throughout the term of my inquiry, but also because I have used it to keep myself on track during the preparation of this work.

So how does marijuana work? My tentative interpretation used to be that it acted chemically in the brain to produce other chemicals somehow associated with feeling high. However, I never accepted the idea that my feelings were the result of chemistry; that was just too mechanical an explanation for me. Scientific research has apparently found that it acts by a mechanism described in Wikipedia as follows: "THC exerts its most prominent effects via its actions on two types of cannabinoid receptors, the CB_1 receptor and the CB_2 receptor, both of which are G-Protein coupled receptors."[37] Whatever *that* means.

In terms of the seer's explanation, chemistry, like everything else physical, is part of the description of the world that we have mistaken for the world itself. If you look at it that way, the chemistry becomes effect rather than cause. If someone were to ask me why I use marijuana, the answer would be that using it judiciously makes me feel better. In fact, I have become convinced that the reason I do anything and everything is that I believe it will make me feel better. That I believe it will make me feel better is also why I want anything

---

[37] http://en.wikipedia.org/wiki/Marijuana

and everything I want. So in terms of my question about how the smoke works, the cause is my desire to feel better, and the effect is the result that the smoke produces. The plant, the pipe, the smoke, and all the other paraphernalia simply constitute the way the Universe arranges things in the world of objects.

There was a time when I used a great deal of the stuff, and looking back I can say that there was considerably more desperation in my wanting than there is now. Back then I didn't realize that I could feel better simply by thinking about something that didn't produce whatever bad feeling I was trying to overcome.

I will also note that cannabis used medically has several well-documented beneficial effects. According to Wikipedia, among these are: "the amelioration of nausea and vomiting, stimulation of hunger in chemotherapy and AIDS patients, lowered intraocular eye pressure (shown to be effective for treating glaucoma), as well as general analgesic effects (pain reliever)."[38] When my first wife Christine decided to have her cancer treated by the medical profession, cannabis is what got her through her bouts with chemotherapy. Without it, I'm clear that the last part of her life here would have been much less comfortable.

LESSONS FROM CHRISTINE

Christine also showed me something else, albeit indirectly, that became part of the new explanation I was trying to develop for myself. From what I understood to be a spiritual point of view, Christine did everything right. She believed deeply in the knowledge our guru had introduced us to. She practiced her meditation regularly, she enthusiastically prepared us for our trips to see him, she attended meetings of his followers regularly, and she endeavored to live what she considered to be a spiritual life. This included what many of his followers considered the right way of eating, which was a vegetarian diet free of preservatives, additives, and all the rest. She and I made several road trips between California and Colorado in the late 1970s, and

---

[38] Ibid.

I can say that being a vegetarian on the road between Santa Barbara and Aspen was not easy during that period.

After Christine was diagnosed with cancer and before she submitted to the medical establishment, she tried mightily to heal herself naturally. In keeping with the thinking of the time, this largely involved diet, supplements, and the like. She also enrolled herself in an in-house program that included counseling and strict adherence to a macrobiotic diet. She wanted very much to get better, but none of these methods seemed to be beneficial for her. After she passed away, I was left with having to make some sense out of all of this. It took many years, but what I believe she showed me was that actions we take in the physical world are like heavy lifting: There's nothing wrong with action, but actions contain no leverage. Relying on actions to allow us to feel better sometimes works, but reversing the process and changing our feelings first is much more effective.

Another way of saying this might be that it's not about what I eat; it's about how I feel about what I eat, how I feel about my body, and how I feel about myself. I have tried to take that lesson to heart. What I continue to find is that if I stop trying to avoid missing the boat, if I stop trying to do everything right and just focus on thoughts that feel good when I think them, I find myself eating sensibly and preferring natural food. On the other hand, trying to eat sensibly in the hope that it will make me feel good just doesn't seem to work. I don't pretend to know Christine's path in life, or what the factors were that made transitioning back to the nonphysical the path of least resistance, but I know in my heart that "doing life right" doesn't make one happy.

DISTINGUISHING THE DOMAIN OF EXPERIENCE

Earlier I made the statement that our entire linguistic inventory arose to deal with the domains of doing and having, in other words, events and objects. That's true of the mind as well.

The mind was not designed to deal with the domain of being. And those who subscribe to the theory of natural selection could say that there's no survival value in knowing about being. What the mind is good at is dealing with records of past experience and the units of meaning ascribed to that experience.

I also spoke earlier of knowledge without language, or direct knowing, as a subtle kind of awareness that emerges when the internal dialog is allowed to die down. Knowing without language is distinct from our usual sense of knowing, which we think of as understanding. Understanding exists in the domain of thought, of the internal dialog. *The Encarta Dictionary* defines understanding in terms of grasping meaning, knowledge of a particular subject, interpretations of things, and so on. Understanding is lives in that aspect of awareness called rationality. Werner called understanding the "booby prize."

In terms of the story our culture tells us about who we are, rationality is very important. Rationality is about figuring things out. In our culture, rationality is very highly regarded; you can see that regard in the word "irrational," which usually carries a derogatory meaning. Don Juan, however, calls rationality, or reason, puny. He makes it clear that rationality is only effective within the bounds of its natural domain, which is to sort through the elements of our inventory, of our explanation of the world. "It craps out," as he put it, when faced with questions that lie outside of that domain. Knowing without language, on the other hand, never fails us, because everything that has ever been imagined or that has ever been understood is held by and within the Universe, the consciousness that we really are. So to borrow a phrase from Werner Erhard, we live in a collapsed domain in which two different kinds of knowing are no longer distinct from one another.

What I've found is that when I spend some time practicing being aware without the internal dialog, thoughts do arise spontaneously, but these thoughts are of a different nature than rational ones; they have a different quality. Our real Selves, gradually revealed as we practice quieting the internal dialog, also have thoughts. But the thoughts of our inner beings are exciting and life-giving, because they represent new possibilities, and new possibilities come from who and what we really are.

With this distinction present in our awareness, we can see where our experience really lives. Experience lives in the domain of knowledge without language, which is distinct from thought. For the most part, we're not even aware of our experience, because it so quickly becomes memory. To really experience, to savor experience, you actually have to postpone the turning of the experience into a memory. That's why the seer's explanation—as well as mystics and seers through the ages—place such a premium on quieting the internal dialog. When Baba Ram Das wrote *Be Here Now*, he was talking about the possibility of living in one's experience instead of living in the memories of the experience. Werner said that living in one's memories of experience is like driving with your attention, and your hands, glued to the rear-view mirror. You have a lot of accidents that way.

THE PROPER USE OF EFFORT

I have already spoken of one of the lessons my first wife Christine taught me, which was that actions are much more powerful when they're leveraged by first changing our feelings. What I've noticed is that when I act in the world from rationality, from trying to figure things out and make things happen, action contains the quality of effort. And in a world where every action provokes an equal and opposite reaction, it takes a great deal of effort to change anything.

So is effort somehow wrong, or is it just misplaced? In this formulation, leveraged action is much more powerful than unleveraged action, and the leverage comes from changing your feelings to those that are a closer match to those your inner being, your real Self, feels. It follows then that the best use of effort is to quiet the internal dialog. To continue the metaphor, don't expend your effort lifting the rock; expend it getting the lever in place instead. The effort to remember to do this, to practice meditation, to practice don Juan's right way of walking, or any other technique you find useful, pays off in ways unimaginable to the rational mind. You could even say that leveraged action, stemming as it does simply from wanting to find a way to feel better, tends to threaten the rational mind. It can feel like an attempt to put the rational mind out of business, which may account in part for the need to practice these techniques with such a great deal of consistency.

ABOUT RIGHT AND WRONG

Right and wrong have presumably been fixtures of culture since the beginning of civilization. People may disagree about which actions fall in these categories, and we often do quite vociferously. But that right and wrong exist as qualities of action is rarely disputed. Right and wrong are intimately connected to meaning; if it turns out that there is no meaning to life other than what an individual human places on it, then right and wrong live not in our actions but in the story we tell about them.

Please note that this argument is not license to act randomly or inappropriately. I am inclined to interpret the tenacity with which we humans have held on to culturally prescribed standards of behavior as indicating that we consider them essential to our survival. In the West, at least, these standards have been passed down to generations for thousands of years. The ability to distinguish right from wrong is used as a legal standard of sanity, after all.

I am also not advocating that standards of right and wrong should be eliminated from culture. Rational beings are very much in need of agreed-upon standards of behavior and the rules and laws with which theses standards have been codified. I say that because when rationality is not seen to be distinct from knowledge without language, rational people have nothing for guidance except the story we tell ourselves about how to behave in the world. But knowledge without words, or the knowledge inherent in direct experience, provides an entirely different and vastly more powerful means of identifying and living by appropriate behavior.

This discussion, when put in those terms, is very much like our earlier look at what and how to eat. It seems to be very difficult to let go of rational strategies and trust that we each have a real Self, an inner being that is a unique expression of an all-knowing Universe. This real Self, who we really are, has a complete and perfect knowledge-without-language of what to think and do in every conceivable situation. I promise that if any such seeker wishes to experience the joy and satisfaction of living in harmony with the rest of the Universe, one has only to step off the edge of the precipice and allow immense relief to replace the fear of doing it wrong, of making a critical mistake. You can practice this with a zip-line as I described earlier, or in meditation in the comfort of your own home, or in any of the myriad daily decisions that one makes. The Universe will meet you halfway, but you have to make the first move. The biblical phrase "Ask and you shall receive" only works in that order.

I've recently come upon a metaphor (yet another metaphor) that I use when I try to grasp knowledge without language. And it lives in my own front yard. I learned some time ago that a grove of aspen trees is often just one organism. When we moved into our house there was just one aspen tree near our front walk. A few years later its root system started to force the concrete up so that it was no longer level. In an effort to stop that, we cut down the tree. The next summer there were hundreds of little aspen trees sprouting on the lawn. We staked out five of them and mowed the rest along with the lawn. We referred to them as the children of the (now gone) original tree, and they're now fully grown, mature trees.

On the surface they look like separate trees, and common sense tells you they are. But knowing about the shared root system allows me to see them as one. And since they are one, they share whatever knowledge trees have about how to flourish, which they all do. It's just a metaphor, but it works for me.

SURRENDER, AND THE ILLUSION OF CONTROL

A couple of chapters ago, I related my experience during the est Training when I suddenly became aware that the voice in my head, the one that constantly describes my point of view at every moment, isn't actually my voice. It isn't actually me. It seems that for a human being, that voice is the verbal expression of the personality-self that we created in order to cope with the inevitable feelings of powerlessness that we experienced as children. Our minds do their best to control the circumstances of life in order to optimize our life experience; they continually advise us which choices to make to maximize wellbeing while minimizing discomfort, failure, and even the threat of dying. That's their design function.

Of course, from the perspective of the seer's explanation wherein in world we perceive is just a reflection of our beliefs, a reflection of the story we tell about our lives, there is no hope of controlling the circumstances of life. You can't control the appearance or disappearance of that pimple on your forehead by doing anything to the mirror. Similarly, you can't control the events portrayed on the screen at the movies by running up to the front of theater. So by identifying with the "voice in our heads," as we all do, we have the illusion of control over the conditions we encounter as we go about our days.

When I had my gas-tank experience in 1974, I heard a voice that I had no choice but to recognize as coming from somewhere else. That voice was as different from the one I listened to every day as it could be. At the same time, I considered myself a follower of that young guru I told you about. I had some grasp back then of the futility of trying to control my life as well as of the possibility that a "higher power" might be a better bet. And the word we followers used at the time was "surrender," surrender of our illusory and obviously ineffectual control.

I had not yet made the distinction I call the real Self, and thus I conceived of surrender as being directed toward someone or something outside of myself. For many of us, the obvious focus of that desire to surrender was the guru himself, in whom we recognized the presence of some power beyond our comprehension. In my case, I believed that a higher power was guiding my life and delivering the perfect sequence of experiences to further my spiritual growth. As this feeling grew in me, I came to feel that the right way of living was to surrender to the whole of my experience and live each moment as it occurred as if it was designed and delivered by that higher power, which I believed at the time was outside of myself.

What's missing in that understanding of so-called higher power, how-ever, is any responsibility for my own experience. While it felt good to relinquish control, which wasn't working anyway, that immature idea of surrender was essentially giving up my own innate power to choose and to learn from my own choices. Additionally, since our world is one in which suffering and all manner of bad (i.e., undesirable) stuff seems so prevalent, the notion of surrender or unquestioned submission to all events, which I now think of as resignation, is clearly not what we had in mind when we chose to enter into this time-space reality.

But in my mid to late twenties, that understanding wasn't at all clear to me, and a particular event occurred that is burned into my memory as the end of my spiritual innocence. There was in my life during that time an older man who was for many years influential in my expe-rience. We often engaged in long conversations about political and philosophical issues, and I valued his insights and opinions. After one of these conversational encounters, however, he made a pass at me. This man obviously wanted to engage in sexual behavior and actually tried to initiate such activity, and I was completely unpre-pared to deal with that kind of experience.

Not only had I never even imagined engaging in homosexual activity, and had no idea what an appropriate response might be, I was also paralyzed by this notion of surrender. This paralysis was so complete that I was unable to respond or react at all, and he finally gave up and left the room in a huff. It was obvious to me that I was being given a life lesson, but my interpretation of that lesson is today radically different. It is, in my understanding, not at all spiritual to unquestion-ingly submit to every experience that comes my way. It certainly is not unspiritual to have boundaries, to say, "No." I believed back then that other people could affect, and potentially determine, my experience. That, as I see it, is why I felt I had to feed that story, that racket, about avoiding being alone and helpless by making other people, especially bigger or older ones, feel sorry for me.

I now see the Universe, and in particular the world I perceive, as reflex-ive. In other words, it reflects back to me the story I tell about who I am, the one I believe in. Other people come into my experience to play their roles in illustrating my story, and I do the same for them. No one can assert himself or insert his intentions into my experience except as his contribution to my growing awareness that I am who I say I am.

So the story I tell today about that experience, distasteful as it was, is about a fledgling seeker struggling to understand that the proper object of surrender for a human being is not to anything or anyone outside oneself. The desire to live in peace and joy, rather, matures with the acceptance of and surrender to who I really am, to my passion, my dreams and, as don Juan said, to "any path that may have heart." My story today is about giving my entire being to this marvelous journey of self-discovery with my family, friends, and loved ones. That's my passion, my path with heart. And I, too, travel, looking and feeling, breathlessly.

THAT "DOWN" ECONOMY

This would be a good time to revisit the topic of the economy, both domestic and global, from the vantage point of the seer's explanation. Start from the premise that what you really are is an individual expression of the Universe, the all-knowing all-that-is, the energy that creates this and all other worlds. There is a real you, but it's not a separate self from who you think you are. That real you is not merely a *part* of who you are, competing with who you think you are for the title of "most powerful" or "most influential." Your inner being is conscious energy, and energy is all there is. All manifestations that we think of as the physical world, while certainly real to us, are actually a product of and held in place by our attention. Our attention is focused on the description of those manifestations, an interpretation of what these elements of the physical world mean to us, and an explanation of why the world appears to us as it does.

So what is an economy? The word, of course, points to an abstraction— no one has ever seen an economy the way we see tables and chairs. The word "economy" points to an abstraction with which we can grasp the totality of a system in which goods and services are exchanged for value received. The seer's explanation says that all goods and services, as well as all other objects and events, are interpretations. We use these interpretations to make sense of the enormous complexity of sensory stimuli—visual, auditory, tactile, etc.—by grouping the stimuli into units and thus identifying objects and events.

We are all members of a culture that has defined the terms of this exchange with ideas like value and worth. Virtually all of us have learned to agree on the elements of this interpretation, and we can therefore identify and measure economic flow, what amounts to the circulatory system of the body of information we think of as the world. We don't have to think about this abstraction called the economy. In fact, we don't. We just use it because we all agree on its meaning. We have developed a symbol, called money, to represent the quantity of this flow, to measure it, and frankly, to keep score.

So, a down economy is one in which economic flow has slowed down or been restricted. Now, we all want stuff; in a down economy, it's not wanting that becomes restricted. Nor does the available supply of stuff become restricted; there is no shortage of stuff on the shelves of any store I've been in recently. What shows up as restricted or limited is only the dynamics of the flow of goods and services, how the exchange of stuff flows. What causes this restriction? Using the metaphor of the circulatory system, what causes the blockage of the veins and arteries?

Because an economy, being an abstraction, is ultimately a story, the elements of the economy I've just described are functions of description, interpretation, and explanation. So the blockage doesn't live in the domain of experience; rather, it lives in the domain of thought and belief. This domain of thought is related to the domain of experience in the same manner as snapshots and memories are related to the scenes they record. This assertion may bring some readers up short. Don't we experience deprivation and lack of opportunity? The seer's explanation says that we do not. Deprivation and lack of opportunity (or lack of anything else) live in the story we tell about the events that take place in our experience. To be sure, hunger and thirst, as well as feeling too hot or too cold, are experiences. It's just that what causes those experiences, or what we think those experiences say about us or the world we live in, belongs to the domain of thought and belief.

Two more elements are crucial to this discussion. The first of these is to reiterate and summarize how our hopes and dreams find their way into our experience. Earlier, I mentioned the idea that our inner Beings, who we really are, are always present in our awareness, even if we are focused doggedly on some aspect of our experience that we don't like. As we focus on these undesirable aspects, our inner Beings, all-knowing as they are, know immediately what sort of experience we would prefer and set in motion the marshalling of people and circumstances compatible with those preferred experiences. To borrow again an image from Esther Hicks, this improved experience is carried on a different vibrational frequency than the one it replaces. It's as if you're watching television, and you're not particularly enjoying the program you've tuned in. To find one you might like better, you have to tune to the channel it's on. Not only that, it's as if your dissatisfaction with the program you're watching sets in motion the production of a replacement television program. Now both programs are being broadcast, but they're on different channels.

One way to think about reaching for this higher frequency—higher on the scale of feeling, not more spiritual or higher on any other scale of judgment—is to alter your expectations. If you believe in Murphy's Law, for example, you will probably expect that at some point things will go wrong. Then when they do, your belief is justified. But if you stalk your power, if you look for evidence that simply thinking thoughts that feel better will produce better-feeling experiences, you will gradually feel yourself accept that you are worthy of that better-feeling experience. And you will then find yourself having higher expectations. In other words, the manifestation of our desires is tempered by what we expect and what we can accept.

The final element in this discussion is that according to the seer's explanation, each of us creates our own experience. The Universe, by virtue of having a virtually infinite range of choices for how to accommodate each of us in our expectation-tempered wanting, does this so seamlessly that it appears "for all the world" as if there is only one world. But in this new explanation there are as many worlds as there are individual expressions of the consciousness that we are. So there are also as many economies as there are us humans. Now, most of us have managed to agree that we are currently living in a down economy (as of this writing, of course.) Why would we do that, given that we feel so much frustration and angst when we observe the gap between what has manifested for us and what we want?

The answer to the question of why we would restrict access to the resources we need is that the restriction somehow validates our limited idea of ourselves. And in the process it serves to perpetuate our racket. It serves to justify decisions made in the domain of thought that have consequences in the domain of experience.

What I have found, after much inquiry, is that in my mental landscape, abundance is sometimes associated with resentment and suspicion, and thinking about abundance brings up a lot of internal chatter about issues of whether one has earned it, whether one deserves it, what it means, what others might think, and whether it has to be protected and defended. In the context of a universally accepted cosmology or explanation that affords a prominent place to the notion of scarcity, relative abundance places one apart from friends and family in the domain of interpretation. And most of us built our personalities, our "acts," in the service of fitting in, of belonging, of not feeling alone. As a result, sudden abundance can feel uncomfortable. In our common sources of information, such as newspapers and television news, stories of lottery winners having a less-than-noble response to their winnings are not uncommon.

What we're left with is that the blockage of economic flow lives in the domain of an individual human being's description and interpretation of the world he or she perceives. That's why there are people who thrive in every bad economy, and there are people who suffer in every good one. There *is* no domestic or global economy; the seer's explanation says that the existence of a single economy is in fact a superstition. For a real Self, for who we really are, there is no blockage of any kind; blockage, in the sense we've been using the word, can only arise in the mind of an individual who has forgotten who he or she really is. Blockage in this context is a function of a belief in scarcity; if a resource is scarce, someone or something can block access to it. But if a resource is not scarce, if it is in fact everywhere, it cannot be blocked. Blockage, or restriction, lives in the domain of thought, of memory, of the description of the world. So when we look at a down economy, we are actually looking at the manifestation of a collective amnesia; we have all forgotten who and what we really are.

That we are collective amnesiacs is the bad news. The good news is that for you to move from the experience of scarcity to the experience of plenty, nobody else has to change a thing. You change your idea of who you are, and the Universe will, over time, effortlessly and seamlessly accommodate you. Other people will no doubt eventually notice the difference, and they will think whatever they think about that. You may find some people drifting out of your experience and others drifting in. I can say it's an amazingly good feeling when you sense your power to live your dreams, especially insofar as they appear to require money to manifest themselves. What before appeared to require a great deal of effort to overcome appears as a wonderful adventure in which you never know where the next delightful surprise will show up.

There is one more fortuitous aspect to looking at the shift from scarcity to abundance from the seer's perspective. You don't have to do it all at once. Earlier, we talked about the idea of stalking oneself. We considered the possibility of viewing the world as a mysterious, unfathomable place where magical things can show up, things that we ordinarily don't notice because we already know what the world is and how it operates. Most of us have no real experience of magical occurrence. I can say, however, that if you make the effort to even be willing to change your idea of yourself and the world, the Universe will meet you more than halfway. You don't need to stop the world, as I did that one day with my gas tank. Just look for clues, and expect to find them. It's well worth the effort.

WHILE WE'RE AT IT – WHAT ABOUT FINANCIAL INDEPENDENCE?

I heard someone the other day talking about wanting to be financially independent. And I wondered, what would that mean in the context of the seer's explanation? For me, the phrase conjures up images of having: having lots of money, income, investments, financial instruments and the like. And of course, that brings up questions about how much is enough, what about inflation and the ups and downs of markets, etc.

It seems to me that looked at from the conventional explanation of who we are and what the world is, there's a lot to consider before one can declare oneself financially independent. From that perspective, we live in a world which exhibits a great deal of uncertainty. Businesses come and go, and some make it and some don't. Some promises get kept and others don't. Expectations are met, or not. In a world in which there's only enough "stuff" to go around, or, in a word, where stuff is scarce, we are forced to compete with one another, and the actions of others can impact what we are able to gather up and how much of that we are able to retain.

That's the conventional interpretation of reality: the "stuff" of life is real, and there's only so much of it, and so we have to strive to gain more, and to protect what we have. The seer's explanation, on the other hand, turns that interpretation of reality upside down. Yes, the stuff of life is real, but it's not as real as we are. Is there another way to look at the idea of financial independence, one in which things aren't so uncertain?

I think the way to answer that question is to look at what I really want. Do I really want lots of money (i.e. large numbers on a screen or piece of paper issued by a bank or similar institution), or do I really want the life experience that I believe those large numbers will bring me? When I get right down to it, what I really want is to *feel* independent, free to make the choices I wish to make, unfettered by the feelings associated with statements such as "I can't afford that."

And here's where the seer's explanation comes in handy: it says that the world shows up in accordance with the story I tell about my life. Can I really just start telling a different story, one in which many of my oft-declared financial limitations don't appear? Yes. Certainly, it requires a great deal of practice to do that. But I'm not alone when I practice. I am an expression of Universal intelligence. I don't have the answers about how to get from scarcity to abundance. But Universal intelligence does. Actually, it already knows how to get me from here to there. So what's in the way? What's in the way is all my beliefs to the contrary.

What if I could really accept that whenever I fully commit myself to follow a given path the resources required to fulfill that path will appear? That would be true financial independence. It doesn't require having anything but what I need at the moment. It doesn't require large numbers of people (i.e. markets) to behave in any particular manner. And it doesn't require any certainty besides the certainty with which I know who I really am.

ILLNESS AND THE BODY AS INDICATOR

I think a fair warning is in order: This section may stir strong feelings of resistance. As counterintuitive as it may sound, we human beings seem to be very attached to our illnesses, our bodily conditions, and our diagnoses. In terms of the way we relate our stories to one another at the local diner, these topics are very often the first to be brought up. It may be that this aspect of shared experience makes us feel not alone at a deep level. In one sense these stories may feed our victim rackets; the sympathy our tales of woe engender seems to be very compelling. In another sense, they are the result of, and serve to mask, feelings we would prefer not to face. If you consider yourself or someone close to you to have an illness or unpleasant diagnosis, I urge you to pay attention to your feelings as you read the following paragraphs.

In the previous section we looked from the point of view of the seer's explanation at the causes of blockage in the flow of money through the economy. It should be relatively easy to move from a discussion of the metaphorical economic circulatory system to the one that moves blood throughout our bodies, and to such difficulties that may restrict the flow of that system and of all other bodily systems. The problem in doing so is a function of the morass of attitudes and opinions and judgments we all have about our bodies. But here again, you can make progress by taking small steps and watching for agreement from the Universe.

First of all, you don't go from a ninety-eight-pound weakling to Charles Atlas overnight (there's a pop-culture reference for you). Everyone knows you have to gradually build up your strength by determined practice. I will note that this is one of the rare examples of a concordance between what "everybody knows" and the seer's explanation. I spoke earlier of the lag the Universe presents between our visualization of a desired or undesired result and the actualization of that result. That's just an aspect of the platform we inherited when we chose to show up in this time-space reality. In physics, that phenomenon is called inertia. The same lag will probably apply if you experiment with addressing a health issue by changing your idea of your body.

Remember Werner Erhard's description of the vicious circle, in which our opinions and judgments tend to shape our experiences, and our experiences tend to reinforce our opinions and judgments. He used the word "vicious" because in the normal course of events, having grown up in this culture, the content of our lives tends to devolve into more and more evidence supporting Murphy's Law, which is about things going wrong. If you were to look at that devolution as tending toward more disorder, you would see that it's just the Second Law of Thermodynamics in action.

But you can just as well have the mirror image of the vicious circle, using whatever adjective you might choose (in a recent issue of *Rolling Stone Magazine*, President Obama is quoted as suggesting "virtuous circle"). I suggest avoiding the temptation to consider the largest physical issue that may have your attention, and focus instead on something relatively minor. If you change some aspect of the story you tell about yourself, and the Universe responds by giving you an indication that you're on the right track, you gain a measure of confidence with which you can shift some slightly larger aspect of your story, of your idea of yourself. Continuing to explore that process results in a gradual building of momentum toward the full experience of the power that you really do have to express yourself more fully in your life.

The seer's explanation says that before we entered into this time-space reality, we were fully aware of who we are as individual expressions of the Universe, of all-that-is. Then, we each made a conscious decision to grow a physical body so we could participate in the world that we all know. So if our bodies were grown in response to the pure desire to express ourselves, why do so many of us seem to have so much trouble with these bodies? After all, our culture has spawned massive industries dedicated to coping with those difficulties, from the medical establishment to pharmaceuticals to alternative therapeutics and so on. And at times the argument about how all this is to be paid for is thunderous.

Just as in our previous discussion of the source of blockage in the flow of the economic circulatory system, and for the same reasons, consider the possibility that our view of ourselves, the story we tell ourselves about who we are, might be the source of our bodily difficulties. As I said earlier, my proposed explanation of the world we perceive tells us that in the domain of all the physical manifestations that greet us when we open our eyes in the morning, we have postulated and adopted an artificial boundary—called our skin—that separates "us" from "not us." I made the statement that one can lose the human form; we can gradually surrender that artificial distinction and see everything within our view as the expression, the manifestation of the way we have handled energy.

I also suggested earlier that looking from the seer's explanation, trying to change situations or conditions with action in the world is like trying to fix an unwanted image in the mirror without changing what's being reflected. It just doesn't work. If you try that world-as-reflection view, if you experiment with it, you can begin to see that body of yours as an indicator of the state of health of your self-regard. After practicing that viewpoint for a while, I now see that various mild but uncomfortable skin conditions I have experienced in the last few years wax and wane according to my attitude about my life. I find that if there's been a period of time in which I'm relaxed and at ease with respect to my life, my skin tends to clear up and become much less of an issue. But if I get caught up in trying to handle some situation with effort or in trying to convince myself or someone else that I'm right, it tends to flare up again.

This view of the body as indicator, however, is tricky for three reasons. First, it's tricky because of the lag between the easing of my mind and the improvement of my skin. I really have to stay focused and optimistically inclined to see the correlation; it's much easier to speculate about what food I ate or what clothing I wore as the cause of the difficulty. Similarly, there's a lag between getting upset about something and having flare-ups. Because of that lag, I might be sloppy about my thinking, or I might just not bother to clean up my attitude about something. Also, I do make use of physical remedies, such as a steroid cream, to control the flare-ups, and it's a lot easier to attribute improvements to the cream. But if I remember to look at the entire issue from the perspective of the seer's explanation, I see that my body, the cream, and everything else are part of a description and an interpretation of what I perceive, and that the boundary between all three is an artificial one.

The second bit of trickiness has to do with the relationship between our attention and what shows up in our experience. This relationship is at the heart of what Esther Hicks speaks about whenever she calls forth Abraham. We human beings are focusers of energy; we're like the lens in a projector that focuses the beam of light into a sharply defined image on the screen. The Universe, all-that-is, holds within it every thought that's ever been thought, and it is our steadily practiced focus on the thoughts we think that makes things real for us. As a result, our experience becomes a representation of the focus of our attention. As Esther puts it, "You get what you focus on, whether you want it or not." That makes things really tricky. If you focus on some troublesome element of the indicator that your body is, and we can hardly avoid doing that, you're actually giving that element more energy, which causes it to stick around longer. That reminds us of Newton's Third Law of Motion as recast by Werner Erhard: "What you resist persists."

The third tricky part of regarding the body as an indicator of the health of one's self-image is what I referred to at the beginning of this section: the depth and nature of the emotions that may be provoked. I have seen these feelings be so strong as to completely deflect a seeker from the exploration of the seer's explanation. I have become convinced that there is no area of the conventional explanation so tightly held as this idea that the human body is subject to bugs, germs, and various other failure modes *over which we have no control*. Perhaps you, the reader, are feeling these emotions as you read this material.

So how do you most effectively use the body as an indicator of the well-being of your self-image? The first thing you have to do is stop regarding physical "issues" as proof that something is wrong. When I have a skin flare-up, I immediately feel as if I've done something wrong (eaten the wrong thing, worn something that's not good for me to wear, or even thought the wrong thoughts). But the truth is there is absolutely nothing wrong with my body (or anything else for that matter). Referring once again to my gas-tank experience, it turned out that there was nothing wrong with my gas gauge. It actually was telling me what was going on. In fact, from the seer's perspective, everything is working perfectly. As I gain more experience with the seer's explanation, I find that when my body doesn't feel good, I remember more and more quickly that I've been entertaining thoughts that don't serve me, that don't reflect, and that actually deflect, the creative power I really am.

Seen in this light, my struggle with vegetarianism in the 1970s was actually a reflection, a physical in-my-face manifestation of a deeper struggle within. That struggle was a mighty effort I engaged in for most of my life to free myself from the sometimes overwhelming feeling of powerlessness that I felt in early childhood and that I cemented in place with my decision to earn the sympathy of others. After all, nobody feels sympathetic toward a person who demonstrates that he is aware of his own power. Now, I reasoned, if I could find a better way to live, if I could only find the right rules to live by, I was sure that would allow me to feel more powerful and demonstrate to my mother that I had really accomplished something.

And just maybe, the reason our bodies get so much attention, especially when they don't work as well as we might like, is that they allow us to focus on the inappropriateness of our thoughts, as no other element of our experience can. Practice that way of looking at things and you'll find yourself appreciating how the process works, and you may even find yourself loving how supportive your body is in helping you refine your focus.

Again, it's a lifelong process that one goes through. It's not an overnight realization that changes everything. Unless it is, of course, as in the case of the experience with the gas gauge in my car almost forty years ago. That experience did indeed change everything, though it has taken nearly four decades for me to process it into the words I write now. That moment of stopping the world is an experience I would wish on everybody. But even without such a moment, life can change miraculously. You just have, as it were, to keep your eyes open.

AN EXAMPLE OF LITERAL METAPHOR

I have learned that the story I tell about myself is the most important factor in determining the quality of my experience. Specifically, I have noticed that there are times when the Universe offers me a look at striking connections between our language and our experience. What follows is a story about someone else, who shall remain nameless so as to avoid unnecessary embarrassment.

My musical career has allowed me the opportunity to make music with a number of very talented drummers. While on a road gig long ago, this particular fellow developed a huge and extremely painful boil on one of his buttocks. As it would have been for any of us who sit down while making our music, this was a real challenge for him. We scoured the local stores in search of a way to help him out, and we came back with a variety of inflatable rings he could sit on to relieve the pressure.

As this episode reached its peak, he and I had a conversation about what he was feeling. While I don't remember much of what was said, we considered the possibility that the boil somehow represented some thought or feeling he was not aware of but that was dominating his experience. At one point he said, "I guess I have been considering myself to be a pain in the ass." Within minutes he looked at me with his face full of relief and told me that the boil had burst.

This was a great lesson for both of us. Not only were we given a glimpse of the connection between the story we tell and our resulting experience, but we also were shown that the Universe can have a rather outrageous sense of humor. Of course, to appreciate that humor, you have to be in the right frame of mind, which is to say you have to somehow transcend our habitual tendency to consider every experience as either a blessing or a curse.

ABOUT THE DEATH EXPERIENCE

I referred in an earlier chapter to my observations of my first wife Christine as she approached the end of her stay in this time-space reality. It was clear to me that she was finding both clarity and comfort during those periods of time when she lay unconscious in her hospital bed. Both were on clear display on that one occasion when she opened her eyes and spoke to me. That experience left me with the certainty that where we came from, and where we will go when we leave here, is both comforting and enlightening (in the sense that our human confusion will be dispelled.)

Christine's passing was not, to my knowledge, an especially difficult or painful one. The same was true for my mother who, with a peaceful look on her face, scrunched up her eyes as if gathering the courage to jump and took her last breath. I have read stories of Native

Americans who, intuiting that their time had come simply walked off into the forest and were never seen again. It is at least part of our stereotypical image of native cultures that children are taught to feel and consider themselves to be part of nature, and they are taught that birth and death are natural processes and are not to be resisted.

Don Juan, who acknowledged his heritage as a Yaqui Indian, told Carlos that a man or woman of knowledge could experience an "alternative way of dying," wherein the practitioner simply assembled another world and disappeared from this one, leaving no trace. In fact, he told Carlos he was convinced that entire societies disappeared from this world in that fashion, a passage that reminds me of the abandonment of prehistoric villages such as Chaco Canyon in New Mexico. Carlos tells us that in the process of demonstrating the "force of alignment," don Genaro, one of don Juan's cohorts, walking ahead of Carlos on a deserted street, once simply disappeared like a "puff of air."

For others, however, we all know that the end (of this lifetime) can be excruciating. What, we may well ask, makes the difference? I well recall how my father suffered in the months and hours leading to his leaving the world. I remember him as a committed atheist and as far as I know completely lacking in spiritual understanding. I remember him as a self-described victim of the McCarthy era, struggling to reconcile his beliefs in the essential goodness of his fellow man with the behavior of specific individuals who appeared to adversely affect his well being. I also recall hearing of the demise of a good friend of mine who was very angry at society and the government, and perhaps the world, after the events of September 11, 2001, and who apparently had a very difficult time in his last days.

What would the seer's explanation have to say about the nature of our death experience? I, of course, have no personal experience of this particular aspect of life. Anecdotal evidence, however, leads me to suspect that those of us who are more accepting of, and less resistant to, our experiences will have an easier time relinquishing these bodies. I fully intend to hold myself up as a test case, for the observation of others, when the time comes.

POLITICS AND THE NATURE OF FREEDOM

People whose rational minds were nurtured in this culture of ours—and I certainly include myself in this category—have learned to view our society as dysfunctional and our world as in desperate need of repair. We see innumerable problems in both our society and our world, and many of us feel a strong need to exert effort in finding and implementing solutions. We see our range of approaches to these problems as living in the domain of action, and we sense (correctly) that the power of action, especially for individuals, is limited. So we identify with groups, often political parties, whose size seems to give us more leverage. Then, either we see ourselves as members of the political persuasion that happens to be in power at present, or we identify ourselves as members of the current minority. In either case, we tend to feel righteous about our ideas, and defensive and antagonistic toward others.

One of the central threads of this often-heated discussion we tend to have is a misunderstanding about the nature of freedom. Most of us agree that freedom is a positive aspect of life, and bondage, its opposite, is a negative. But when freedom is thought about in rational terms, the conversation about freedom becomes an argument about which of the limited range of options afforded by the current possibility should be public policy. What restrictions, if any, should be placed on the behavior of individuals or groups of individuals? When do such restrictions, when put in place in "the public interest," become undue impediments to the individual's right (and imperative) to choose?

Because we identify ourselves as rational beings, and because the effectiveness of rationality is confined to its rather limited domain— that of thoughts that are allowed by the current explanation—we are forced to think of freedom as being something that is relative, under attack, or just missing. In other words, we believe in the scarcity of freedom. In terms of the current political debate, either our freedom appears to be threatened by some other person or group's idea of fairness, or our freedom seems to have been taken away by an unfair distribution of wealth and power.

Because we believe so strongly in scarcity, which is an inevitable logical result of seeing ourselves as objects among objects, everything we value in life is seen to be in finite supply. This gives rise to life as a zero-sum game, in which if you get more of something we both value, I must then get less. This applies to money, desirable objects, potential lovers or mates, good jobs, and on and on. If I believe I have some power to exert (this kind of power would more properly be called force,) and if I see another group of people as competing with me for what I value, I may well try to use that power to force them to live within certain boundaries that keep them away from me and my territory. And, of course, the reverse is also true. Obviously that's been going on as long as we have been human beings; in fact, that sort of competition is wired into most animal species, including ours.

But the seer's explanation says that the idea that we are objects among objects is a superstition. It says instead that we are perceivers who interpret sensory stimuli according to the rules of an interpretive system; it is that interpretation that contains the idea that we are objects. If you try that explanation on for size, you may see that there are no objects "out there" that can affect our freedom. Who we really are is completely free, and the only way for bondage to show up in our experience is to habituate ourselves to beliefs and patterns of thought that incorporate bondage. Quoting Esther Hicks once again, "You are so free you can choose bondage."

The seer's explanation further says that what each of us sees as the world is actually our own description of the world, and the Universe, with its virtually infinite range of possibilities, blends everyone's description together into a coherent whole that, as I said earlier, is so seamless that we don't even notice that we've mistaken the description of the world for the world itself. With that explanation in mind, we can see that no other person can assert himself into our experience. My experience is a function of the interpretation of the sensory input I perceive—and the world I create as a result—and of that interpretation alone. Going back to my first example in this chapter, if I see the world as a dangerous place (i.e., if that's my interpretation of the world I perceive), it's entirely possible, even probable, that someone may appear whose intentions could appear dangerous to me.

But in the seer's explanation the idea of danger rests upon believing that we are objects among objects. If we come to see that interpretation as a superstition, danger evaporates as an interpretation as well. Without danger as a feature of our description of the world, people with "dangerous" proclivities either will not manifest those proclivities in *our* experience, or they simply will not show up while we're around. If you can free yourself from the idea that there is one world we all are stuck with, you will see the bad stuff in the world for what it is: It's a manifestation of energy consistent with the expectations on the part of the people who experience it.

People show up in my experience in accord with the way I see myself and my world. As I said earlier, we are all capable of showing up in multiple vibrational modes. I know, for example, that I am capable of a wide range of moods and attitudes, and I'm pretty sure everyone else is too. So when someone enters my experience, they will tend to show up for me in a manner consistent with my general mood. Seen in that light, I'm the one controlling what sort of people appear in my experience.

TELEVISION, THE NEWS, AND THE DEFAULT EXPLANATION

There is, I think, a strong argument for weaning ourselves from a preoccupation with the news. Someone who watches or reads the news with any consistency may well come to feel that the world is terribly broken. They will probably also acquire a very cynical attitude about the motivations and inclinations of other people. Some people may think of the news as simple information, and watching it as exercising the responsible person's obligation to stay informed. But the news isn't just information. In our culture it's always prepared within a particular explanation, within a particular view of the world, and it's delivered from a particular perspective. And finally, it isn't complete; it doesn't begin to cover the full range of how people are handling energy our world.

We might have thought that the shift from the half-hour news shows we had in the 1960s to the so-called twenty-four-hour news cycle would have vastly expanded the scope of coverage, and many people believe that's what actually happened. But the news actually represents a viewpoint, the viewpoint of the "Tonal of the times," the predominant explanation with which the vast majority of people operate their knowledge of the world. The expansion of the availability of news has only enlarged the inventory of manifestations of that viewpoint, not the range of viewpoints or the scope of any particular one. And the seer's explanation says that the dominant viewpoint in the world today is what makes the world show up as it does for all of us who share that viewpoint.

If you watch network (commercial) television, you are subjected not only to the news and its clear orientation toward the problems of the world, but also to the commercials themselves. Some of these are relatively innocuous, though they do continue the exposure of viewers to endless reiterations of the dominant worldview; some are even great fun, as evidenced by the shows devoted to them around Super Bowl time. But some pointedly serve to perpetuate feelings of negativity regarding the nature of the world. Witness the commercials for security services, insurance companies, lawyers (in particular those with a specialty in injury or tort law), and so on. Commercials for weight-loss products tend to get viewers focused on their current physical shape and size, rather than the results for which the products are marketed. And the winner of the rub-your-nose-in-it sweepstakes may be ads for prescription medications, which serve to remind us of how many ways the body can go wrong.

It seems to me that the news, and the commercials most people wind up watching, play a central role in the perpetuation of the world's problems that we spoke of earlier in this section. We continue to focus on the ills of the world, whether it be political dysfunction, poverty, illness, climate, the plight of animals, and on and on, and the only thing that really changes is that we feel worse and worse. It is the continued focus of our attention that causes a particular configuration of energy to show up as experience.

I invite you to consider the possibility that if you withdraw your attention from acting on the feeling that you need to stay informed about the world, and instead focus consistently on what brings you joy and good feelings, the world *you* experience will morph into one that is more to your liking. If you do the work necessary to change your viewpoint in that way, the community you live in will either gradually turn into the one you desire, or you will find yourself with good, logical reasons to find another one that will. And I predict that when that happens, you will hear the clamor of the news, and the political posturing it records, as just so much of what Shakespeare's Macbeth called "sound and fury signifying nothing."

KATHIE

I spoke earlier of my second wife, Kathie, the mother of my son, Luke. While we are no longer married to one another, I can say that she and Christine are among the most special people I have ever known. I met Kathie before this adventure began, or perhaps more accurately, before I became aware of it as an adventure or as the inquiry that's the subject of this book. She was working as an RN in Laguna Beach, California, and I was living in Aspen, just getting started in my career in music. We met through a mutual friend at a time in my life when I wasn't looking for love. In fact, I can say that I have never had anything memorable begin when I was looking for it.

After conducting a long-distance romance for a couple of years, we broke it off simply because we weren't spending enough time together to nurture the relationship and allow it to grow. We did so lovingly and without any of the blame or guilt that might have damaged the relationship. The mutual friend who had introduced us stayed friends with both of us, and after Christine's passing, she informed Kathie of the news. Kathie wrote to me, we spoke on the phone, I paid her a visit, and before we knew it the fire had been rekindled after lying dormant for fifteen years. It wasn't long before she became pregnant with Luke, and we married in late 1987 before Luke was born.

Kathie and I were married for twenty-four years. We raised Luke together and committed ourselves to living as full partners. In retrospect, it appears very much as if Luke brought us back together, having chosen us as parents for what we could each contribute to his life and for the environment we created together in which he grew up.

Of course, that's the story I tell. I could just as easily tell a story about serendipity and luck, but this story just feels better. I'm most grateful to all the teachers about whom I've spoken in this book for the perspective that, when we stop to consider our lives, we find that our thoughts, our memories, and our stories are all we have to work with. Our experiences, rich and profound as they are, are fleeting; they are immediately turned into memories that live in an entirely different domain. As a result, my story about being with Kathie is all I have, and I might as well tell the story in a manner that feels as good as any story I can tell.

Kathie and I had "a great run together," as she put it. We have the memories, and the photos and videos, that demonstrate the joy with which we lived together and raised Luke. When Luke left for college a number of years ago, I think that the glue went out of the relationship. The job was done, the journey together was completed, and we were already moving apart. That's the way I choose to tell that part of the story. In that story there is no blame, no making the other person wrong or at fault. In fact, I'm very proud of Kathie for making the first move, for recognizing at some level that it was time to move on. We were co-petitioners for the dissolution of our marriage, partners in its end as well as its beginning and middle. There's a lyric in John Denver's song "I'd Rather Be a Cowboy" that touches on my feelings about our parting:

> The absence of her laughter is a cold and empty sound
> But her memory always makes me smile
> And I want you to know
> I love her, yes I love her just enough to let her go

When we entered RCA studios in New York to record *River of Love* that day in 1973, John had just finished recording that song, and it was playing back as we walked in. Sometimes things just come around again.

CHAPTER 15

DREAMING, AND HOW WE CREATE OUR REALITY

For years I had a recurring nightmare. In this dream I found myself stark naked in a public place with lots of people around. This experience would always prove highly embarrassing, though no negative consequences ever befell me in the dream. As I gained some degree of proficiency in using the seer's explanation, I came to see that the real experience I had in that dream was the embarrassment I felt, and not the scene played out in my mind's eye that seemed to cause it. It has since become increasingly apparent to me that the people, objects, and events that formed the content of the dream simply constituted window-dressing (i.e., a representation using the elements of my description of the world that was consistent with the emotion I was feeling). I wondered if that idea pertained to my "real," waking experience as well.

One night, after years of occasionally suffering through this nightmare, I suddenly became aware that I was <u>dreaming</u> that I was naked on a street corner with lots of people around. I had that realization through what I earlier called knowledge without language; I didn't so much think that I was dreaming as I simply became aware of it. Instantly I was in a car, still naked, driving away from the scene, aware that being in the car implied that I was both shielded from view and also removing myself from anyone who may have seen me naked. This was a case of what is called "lucid dreaming," a phenomenon in which the person, while having the dream, becomes aware that he or she is dreaming. As far as I remember, I've never had that dream again.

In Carlos Castaneda's later books, there is a great deal of description of what don Juan called *dreaming* (which Carlos always italicized in his writing). He was referring to a sort of advanced lucid dreaming in which the practitioner is not only aware of the dream but learns to consciously control it. Carlos wrote that during his time with don Juan and don Genaro, he observed them many times performing physical maneuvers that would be unthinkable—and were unthinkable to Carlos—in the context of normal human experience.

In his presentation of the sorcerer's explanation, don Juan said that while possibilities exist for people to perform some of these movements in their regular bodies (my reading of the exploits of Harry Houdini come to mind here), a sorcerer's true abilities come to fruition in what he called "the double," which is a body that a sorcerer develops in *dreaming*, and that when perfected can actually appear before, and interact with, the regular bodies of other people. These stories, these "tales of power," are certainly not necessary to grasp and use the seer's explanation, but they are awesome and beautiful stories if one can put aside, even momentarily, "what everybody knows" is possible in the "real world."

I have read descriptions that others have written of experiences in which they have had dreams of flying. Type "lucid dream flying" into an online search engine, for example, and you'll see references to many of these descriptions. Though I have not been privileged to have any of these dreams, it seems clear upon reading about them that the dreamer has the experience of flying. After years of considering these ideas, I have become convinced that the pragmatic difference between the experiences we have in dream awareness (whether lucid or not) and in normal, waking awareness lives not in the domain of experience but rather in the domain of memory.

I have had, as far as I remember, only that one experience of being aware that I was dreaming. In all my dreams, however, the experience I have is as real as when I'm awake. It is only in retrospect, after I awaken, that I realize it was "only" a dream. Sometimes that's a relief; once in a while it's a disappointment. Experience takes place here and now, before the mind has a chance to make a multisensory record of it and store it as a memory. The feelings one has when one is dreaming are as real as the feelings one has when awake. In that sense, the dream experience is as real as the waking one; the only difference is that when it is recorded in the mind in that linear sequence, the information that it was a dream is usually included.

The realization that dream experiences are as real as waking experiences *in the domain of experience*, as opposed to the domain of memory, is a potentially important point in trying to grasp the impact of the seer's explanation. We should understand that the first step in this effort is to appreciate that we live in—and from—an explanation of ourselves in which separate domains have collapsed and are no longer distinct. Though most people, I believe, aren't aware of it, experience and memory are truly separate domains, and our attention, as I said before, can only be directed to one or the other in any given moment. But human beings don't typically make that distinction; as I noted before, Werner pointed out that our dissatisfaction with life stems from mistaking the "menu for the meal."

Once one understands and accepts the existence of those separate domains, experience and memory, one can notice which domain one is attending to at any moment. You might think that you can't notice when you're focusing on the domain of experience; certainly, as soon as you think about your experience, you're no longer there. But remember that while most of us believe that knowing and thinking-about are the same, they're not. When you're experiencing, you know that you're experiencing; you can practice being present to your experience and noticing when you have shifted to the domain of memory and are now remembering, thinking about, the experience you just had.

The seer's explanation says that the entirety of the world we experience is actually a description. This description is of increasing complexity as we grow, but it is made of simple building blocks that we learned to perceive as we were taught language, as we were given the words to name objects and basic actions. Each word we were taught was related by our parents and other teachers to a perceived object or scene, and our words came to represent *memories* in which were stored our impressions of those objects and actions.

This is a crucial distinction. *Our words represent memories.* They don't actually name the elements of our experience; when we're experiencing, we're not using words. With regard to our experience, we are knowing-without-language. Rather, our words name the elements of the memories of those experiences.

As we were taught language, we were taught the description of our world at the same time. As we grew, the physical-ness of our world, rich with sensory impressions as it is, literally captured our attention, and we forgot the actual nature of the relationship between our words and our experience. And we came to see our world as what's real, and our words became simply handles with which to interact with the various parts of the world.

Now return to the idea that dream experience is as real as waking experience. In my "naked" dream, for example, my experience consisted of the feeling of embarrassment. The question arises, "How about the people and the street corner in that scene? Were they part of the experience?" I can say that they were, in the sense that my attention was focused on those elements of the dream experience and not on thinking about or remembering the dream experience. Well, were those people and the street corner real? That's a tougher question to answer. They were certainly real when I was "there" (i.e., when my attention was focused on them). But as soon as I woke up, they were no longer "there."

The seer's explanation says that all the elements of my dream were real when I was dreaming, just as it says that all the elements of the coffee shop and its occupants are real as I sit here with my laptop. It further says that each of us is the creator of his or her own reality. Accepting the seer's explanation for the purposes of investigation, I'm therefore led to the seemingly inescapable conclusion that I am creating in its entirety the scene that's playing out before me. Again, what about the other people I can see and hear? Aren't they real? Am I creating them as well? It may sound like a tautology, but obviously who-they-really-are is real. All of us here—and by extension all of us—are co-creators, creating this scene together. (As I typed that sentence, I felt my sense of the world shift; I could glimpse that the separation among all of us here, in which we believe so strongly, is in fact an illusion. We are simply consciousness looking at this scene from different perspectives.)

Continuing to follow this idea wherever it leads, the seer's explanation says that the scene before me, existing as it does in time and space, is only the description of the world, not the world itself, which don Juan called mysterious and unfathomable. So the physical perspectives (i.e., I'm looking at the coffee shop from over here, and she's looking at it from over there) are representations in the domain of thought—the physical description of the world—of different perspectives in the domain of experience. We are each a unique perspective of all-that-is, with a unique combination of feelings and emotions, and our different perspectives are projected and viewed through the filter of different assumptions, memories, etc. When these different perspectives are projected into an agreed-upon world, they show up as separate individuals.

So was the nursery rhyme, the one about rowing your boat, literally correct? Is life "but a dream"? Not if by "dream" you mean something that's not real. There is nothing that is not real about living, about the experience of being alive. It's just that our dogged insistence on thinking of the world as what's real—and the resulting relegation of our experience of it to something more ethereal and fleeting—forces us to place the emphasis where it doesn't belong, and where it doesn't serve us if our intention is to be happy, and that is on the conditions and circumstances we tell ourselves we face. If you focus consistently on the world you think is real, and if you believe your happiness depends upon the particular way the elements of physical reality are arranged, you will be pulled to and fro by the world's unpredictability, the persistent tendency with which the world seems to break down, and its seeming unwillingness to make us happy.

If, on the other hand, you focus consistently on your actual experience, which the seer's explanation says you can only do if you learn to quiet the internal dialog, you will find yourself no longer being pulled from one emotion to another by forces and events you cannot control. You will find the world that you perceive increasingly willing, not so much to make you happy, but to reflect your decision to be happy and satisfied regardless of events, conditions, and especially the actions of other people. You cannot control what other people do, but you can control your experience of what they do (i.e., your reaction to what they do). In fact, you can simply stop reacting at all to what they do, and instead appreciate that what they do represents the best effort of which they are presently capable to be happy and to cope with the lives they lead. Nothing they do is about you; it's all about them.

I've talked about the nature of the "naked" dream I had because it helps to illuminate the seer's explanation. The remaining aspect of that dream is the fact that at the moment I realized I was dreaming the content of the dream shifted. It would be perfectly natural to assume that my presence in the car, hidden from onlookers and moving away from the busy street corner where I felt so embarrassed, caused the sense of relief I felt, the absence of the embarrassment. That is an interpretation that's consistent with our standard way of looking at experience, which is that our experience is a product of conditions and circumstances.

But the seer's explanation says that the causal relationship between experience and conditions actually works the other way around. It says that my realization, my knowing-without-language that I was "only" dreaming, dissipated the feeling of embarrassment because that feeling was no longer operative in that new context, and the world of my dream experience rearranged itself to reflect that change in experience. In other words, something within me knew that, in that dream context, my usual assumption that it matters what other people think of me was no longer relevant and no longer operative, because in a dream such as the one I was having, no one else was present. All there was in my view of the world of the dream was my experience and the window-dressing I had assembled.

And the seer's explanation says that's exactly what happens in waking experience. My actual experience, as distinct from my memories of and thoughts about my experience, is projected into the description of the world that we mistake for the world itself, and that description (the world) shows up with objects and a cast of characters that faithfully reflect and dramatize that new experience, that new knowing. The most significant difference between this case, in which the scene changed immediately in response to my altered experience, and the case of my skin issues eventually improving as a result of my constant efforts to pry my attention away from whatever thoughts, attitudes, and feelings caused my stress, is that in the dream there was no lag. In what our culture would call "real life," there is a built-in lag, as I discussed earlier, between the idea and the physical manifestation in this time-space reality. Physics calls this phenomenon inertia.

There is one more story I will relate in the context of this discussion of what's real and what's not, and it comes again from Carlos Castaneda. In the final chapter of his book, *Journey to Ixtlan*, don Genaro, don Juan's closest companion, relates his story of transformation as a metaphorical journey to return to the Mexican town of Ixtlan. In that story he talks about encountering people and discovering that they are not real but are instead, in his word, "phantoms." It's taken me years to understand what he meant. The people he encounters on that journey are certainly real; they, like you and I, are energetic beings with the human capacity to focus that energy through attention.

But there is a distinction between people who are aware of who they really are and those who are not. Those of us who are not yet aware of ourselves as conscious energy, as the context in which our world shows up, live our lives into the collapsed distinction between experience and memory. When we live into that collapsed distinction, we immediately classify people whom we encounter in terms of a preexisting scheme that is part of our description of the world. In other words, without being aware of it, we instantly search our memories for similar characteristics of people we already know, we remember what those folks are like, and we classify the new person in those terms.

According to the seer's explanation, our personalities—our ways of being in the world—are coping mechanisms designed to avoid being dominated, to avoid being found out as faulty or defective, and to survive. When we go through life believing that we are those personalities, those separate beings, we can be said to be all act, all racket, all story. Those, I believe, are the people don Genaro called, "phantoms."

So it appears that when we're not conscious of being who we really are, we go through life with our attention firmly focused on the past, because memory is the recorded past. I've already quoted one of Werner Erhard's classic metaphors: It's as if we drive our cars through life with our vision firmly fixed on the rearview mirror, and when you do that, "you have a lot of accidents." When we go through life focused on the description of the world, we're focused on memories of past events. So we're focused on the past, and we're not present— present to ourselves, present to each other, present to experience. But the possibility always exists to "wake up," to become aware of who we really are, to make that crucial distinction between experience and memory. Experience is current, or now; memory is past, or then. They are separate domains, and to make that distinction, to quiet the internal dialog and come into the present, is to be truly alive, to be truly real.

CHAPTER 16
THE LAST

If you've read this far, you may have gotten the impression that I'm making the following claim: that adopting the seer's explanation means that one doesn't have to have "negative" experiences, or that all will be sweetness and light. I hasten to assure you that the seer's explanation doesn't insulate us from bad feelings, such as anger, resentment, frustration, and all the rest. But I have found that it does give us a way of holding or considering those feelings when they arise that enables us to allow them to, as it were, enter our experience from one side and exit out the other.

Even more powerfully, these "bad" experiences, in which we become more keenly aware of what we really don't want, allow our real Selves to envision and create what we would prefer, what we do want, and what will allow us to more fully express ourselves as who we truly are as human beings. The story I now tell about myself is that uncomfortable experiences from the past have enabled me to attract and allow new experiences that I find more joyful. What follows is a small collection of personal stories related from where I now stand.

A PERSONAL STORY—RAISED IN THE WORLD OF CLASSICAL MUSIC

I grew up in a family headed by two very competent and accomplished people. Because my father died young, it fell to my mother to do her best to raise me with the values and the understanding about life she felt would be best for me. Mom was blessed with extraordinary talent, and she was pushed somewhat mercilessly by her father, her first violin teacher, to develop that talent. This she did, with unbending intent and commitment, and she made a real mark on her chosen profession, as I have described earlier.

While I also became a professional musician along the way, I have never seen myself as blessed with that same gift. In fact, when I was about four years old, Mom put a small violin in my hands, showed me how to hold it, and showed me how to produce a sound from the instrument. This had been her initiation into the exclusive circle of immensely talented musicians, and she probably expected me to be the next in line. I did try to play that violin, and I have photographs as evidence of that effort. But after a few sessions, she let me know I was off the hook, in the sense that she did not consider me the one to continue the lineage of which she had clearly proven herself to be a member.

I don't recall my reaction to that news at the time. If I were to receive it today, I believe I would feel mostly relief. My understanding is that Mom didn't have much of a childhood, in the sense that practicing six hours a day while attending school is probably more than all but the most dedicated among us would put up with.

I knew from an early age that my mother was a success, and that this particular path to success, called "child prodigy" or "world class," was not going to be available to me. That she was eminently successful was clear to me because of the people with whom she associated and by whom she was professionally accepted, as well as from the accolades she consistently received as acknowledgement for her work. I have photos of her rehearsing and performing with such classical music luminaries as Jascha Heifetz, Gregor Piatigorsky, Igor Stravinsky, and many, many others.

My path through life, as is probably obvious by now, has been quite different. Both my parents were largely focused on developing and sharing their respective musical gifts, and they remained so throughout their lives. I see my path and purpose in this life as having a much broader scope, with much less in the way of tangible accomplishment to show for it. As I became aware of the feelings of confusion and inadequacy I had with regard to this comparison one perhaps inevitably makes between oneself and one's parents, I was forced to find ways to make up for it.

I decided early on that I could not compete with my parents in the area of outward accomplishment. I watched my mother and observed her accumulation of the outward symbols of success: a beautiful house, a rare old Italian violin, modest but significant financial assets, and all the rest. I felt intimidated by her prominence and her apparent power, and in my silent comparisons of the two of us, I never measured up. In the process, I failed to distinguish between her real inner success, which I believe she felt deep within herself, and those outward trappings of success. That misunderstanding, in which I mistook outward expressions for inner realizations, became a deeply ingrained habit, and I believe it has colored every personal interaction I have ever had.

And so, throughout my technical, musical, and political careers, I never felt truly successful. I was always looking in the wrong place: to the external evidence that seemed to always be just out of my reach. I have finally come to the understanding that external evidence generally comes about as an expression of inner knowledge that one is deserving of that external evidence. In my experience, at least, expecting to acquire the appearance of success first, in order to allow me to have the actual experience of success, is putting the cart before the horse.

❧

I spoke earlier of the last interaction I had with my mother, in which I wound up yelling at her. I now see that event as a first, clumsy, and obviously hurtful attempt to regain my power. On the evening I'm speaking of, she was complaining about her loss of mobility and freedom as she entered her early nineties, having decided she shouldn't drive anymore and having given away her car. I responded to her complaints by suggesting she hire a car and driver a couple of times a week. Her immediate and angry reaction to that suggestion was, "Spoken like a rich man's son."

Mom and I had argued for years about my attitude toward money. Her opinion was that I didn't take it seriously enough, and mine was exactly the opposite: that I took it too seriously. Her efforts to make her point once extended to watching me extract a length of dental floss from the container and criticizing me for taking too much. I suspect living through the Great Depression principally shaped her approach to money, and mine in turn was largely a product of having come of age in the 1960s, with its ethos of minimizing the importance of material possessions.

In response to her "rich man's son" comment, I felt a rush of anger arising from deep within myself. My anger was undoubtedly the product of years of resentment focused on the disparity of our relative financial resources and, not incidentally, how hard I felt I had worked to gain her approval and understanding. This resentment in turn was the product of how I viewed this disparity and what I decided it meant about me: that I was not deserving of financial success because I had not selected a skill at an early age and focused on it unwaveringly, as she had.

I suppose that from her point of view she felt she had somehow failed to instill the proper values in me, and perhaps she was attempting to make up for it by trying to correct her mistakes while she still could. I said to trusted friends on numerous occasions that I felt she was still trying to raise me, and I felt that as a result her words reflected barely contained condescension.

If I separate my anger and resentment from my eventual verbal explosion, I see that I was really letting her know that a certain way of speaking to me was no longer acceptable. It was a start, and the process continues. In an abstract sense, regaining one's power seems as if it should be a simple process: just stop giving it away. I have come to see, however, that the people to whom we give our power get attached to having that power. And it appears that they don't want to give it up. To anyone who wishes to try out that point of view, I suggest setting boundaries with respect to someone who appears to be in a position of relative power. Let them know—lovingly and gently, if possible—that certain of their behaviors, which you formerly had tolerated, are no longer acceptable. Then watch how they react.

A PERSONAL STORY—GETTING OVER IT

As I write this section, it's thirty-five years since I left Liberty, the band and the people whom I love dearly and with whom I had so many wonderful adventures. Not long ago, Dan Wheetman wrote to say he and Jerry Fletcher had talked about getting the band back together, and he floated the possibility to the rest of us. My first reaction was that it was a lovely idea. That good feeling was replaced almost immediately by that same gnawing anxiety I felt all those years ago, and which I was certain I had moved beyond. I became involved in a consuming internal debate between a fearful voice that didn't want anything to do with any experiences that might cause me to feel those awful feelings I felt back then, and a "more mature" voice that insisted I had no choice but to face those feelings if I had any chance of coming out the other side relatively intact.

The upshot of that internal debate was that I let the email from Dan sit in my inbox unanswered for weeks. I discussed the issues verbally with Jan, and I felt a small measure of relief at her agreement that there were indeed "real issues." This was followed by a few additional weeks of silence on my part, until she finally wrote to say that if we were going to do a reunion we had to decide because people have schedules, venues have timelines, and all of that. The pressure I felt at that point seemed to leave me with no choice but to hit "reply all" and say I just wasn't into it.

Of course that didn't work either. I received a sweet reply from Dan saying it was all right whatever I decided, and that all he wanted was to experience once again the joy we used to feel. Finally, I forced myself to come face to face with the fact that whatever pain we experience in life, we do it all to ourselves. I'm the one who took whatever words were spoken back in the 1970s—and much earlier by my parents—and had them mean something about me. I was the one who allowed my fear of not keeping up with the band's growth to build upon my memories of trying to convince my mother that I was on the right path, with the result that I decided that I wasn't up to the job. I'm the one who gave up my power in exchange for making dear friends wrong so I could feel justified in my resistance.

What I finally got to was the understanding that what I feel doesn't *mean* anything about me. I simply feel what I feel, and being afraid of feelings is what keeps me from feeling alive and engaged with other people. So I hit "reply all" again, and I acknowledged that I'm "off it," which was to say no longer taking the stand I had earlier announced that I wasn't interested in the reunion, and instead I was ready and willing to participate in whatever comes along. It's embarrassing to acknowledge resistance that strong to people I love. But that's the doorway I have to go through to get to the relief that's on the other side, to get back to feeling powerful again.

THE BOTTOM LINE

So I've come to the essence, the bottom line of this new explanation I am proposing, what I'm calling the seer's explanation. We are not what we think we are, and the world is not what we think it is. The seer's explanation says that the Universe is pure energy. It is all-that-is, all-knowing and intimately aware of everyone and everything that has ever been. It is Self, which is why, in this context, I capitalize the word "Universe." It is pure consciousness, in which all the thoughts and combinations of thoughts that have ever been thought "float like barges," as don Juan once put it. You could say that this pure consciousness exists everywhere and eternally, but space and time are

just ideas that the Universe thought up. That's one of the most difficult things to get about the seer's explanation: There is only here and
now; there is no there or then in the domain of experience. There and
then exist only in the domain of memory.

It may well be, as don Juan said, that the Universe has created more
than one world. Carlos gives a short description of his brief and rather
uncomfortable experiences in what don Juan considered one of the
others, which he called the "Black World." But this world, our world,
is a stable platform the Universe has created for us and upon which
one can have experiences and share them with others. The platform
our world affords us to stand upon is woven of a few fundamental or
primal abstractions. Most fundamentally, these are space and time,
matter, and all the other ideas one encounters in a study of physics,
as well as perhaps the most important abstraction for us humans:
possibility.

This pure consciousness, this Universe, *is what we are*. Each of us is,
in a sense, a unique perspective on the totality of what the Universe
has created. We are each a resonant focusing circuit, able to tune in
or focus on any combination of those floating thoughts and, by consistently focusing on that combination, make it into reality, into real
experience. To play in this world, to stand on the platform, one first
makes a conscious decision to do so, and with great abstract purpose
and intention. One then finds oneself in one of the new bodies being
grown, with physical characteristics and a geographical and social
story best suited to that purpose and those intentions. Naturally, this
new body comes with sensory apparatus and an interpretation mechanism, and with this equipment we make sense (i.e. a world) out of
what would otherwise be a cacophony of sensations.

What would an abstract purpose and intention look like? I really
have no way of knowing what someone else's purpose is in being
here, what they chose for a purpose in entering this time-space reality. In fact, it is only after a great deal of effort that I can state what I
believe mine is. I believe I came here to become a man of knowledge,
to go as far as I can in understanding what it is to be a human being,

and to develop as best I can the ability to convey this understanding to others.

I had a conversation with my dear friend JD Martin one recent morning, during which we were discussing the ideas in this book. As I described the idea that one could shift the ultimate context, the context in which everything else takes place, from the world (i.e., spacetime) to consciousness, he asked me, "Do rocks have consciousness?" As he asked that, I felt the distinction "ultimate context" come into sharper focus. If you consider his question, you see that for something to be said to *have* consciousness, consciousness has to be a quality or an attribute of something realer, more tangible, or more fundamental. For example, if an object is said to have a particular color, the object in question is more fundamental, and the color is an attribute of that more essential reality.

If you are willing, however, to consider the possibility of shifting your idea of "ultimate reality" from the world to consciousness itself, consciousness would then be the more fundamental essence, and as such it could not be merely an attribute of something else. That's an important distinction, since most of us consider consciousness, whether we realize it or not, to be an attribute of certain forms of organic life, just as most of us consider life to be a property of certain kinds of matter.

The seer's explanation says that as individual expressions of pure conscious energy, we make a deliberate tradeoff to come here. What we get is the richness of physical experience. What we trade for that, willingly, and for what is to our real, eternal Selves but a short period of time, is the memory of who we really are. We give up full and complete autonomy, insofar as our personalities are concerned, especially while we are infants; what we get in return is the opportunity to participate in the expansion of the Universe, the expansion of the realm of possibilities, of all-that-is.

Before we come here, and after we leave the planet, we are not participants in, and therefore not subject to the rules of, this time-space reality. But we do have access to all the thoughts that have ever been

THE LAST

thought, and we can synthesize new thoughts at will. Because we are not subject to limitation, lack, scarcity, or inevitability before we come here, all the thoughts we entertain and synthesize are free of those negative attributes, and so we remain in our natural joyful state as Beings. We retain awareness of all others with whom we have shared our time-space experiences, and we retain our interest in all the ideas we were interested in before. And we love all this unconditionally.

According to the seer's explanation, our natural condition as whole, complete beings is to be at peace, at rest. If we turn our attention toward anything, we do so with love. That's why it is said that "God is Love." In this explanation, God is shorthand for the conscious, unlimited energy that we really are. And what we feel, when we are being what we are, is love. Once we are in these bodies, in this time-space reality, we are typically raised by people who are not fully aware of who they are, and so we are essentially forced to accept an explanation of life that incorporates some elements of limitation, lack, scarcity, and inevitability. As we live in this explanation, we tend to feel the feelings associated with those elements, which usually consist of anxiety, frustration, fear, and so on. These are the negative feelings we all feel at one time or another.

But love is not a feeling we have when we acquire the right circumstances, the right friends, the right lovers, the right thoughts. Rather, it is what is left when all the negative feelings are stripped away, because that is what we really are. The return to love always happens when we make our transitions back to the nonphysical, when as physical beings, we die. But it also happens more and more as we retrain ourselves to think thoughts that don't foster negative feelings. And the seer's explanation says that we can recover the knowledge of who and what we really are while still in these bodies and this time-space reality. As Esther Hicks puts it, "You don't have to croak to do that."

Because love is a fundamental aspect of the experience of who we really are, we can see the purpose of a relationship shift. Many of us believe, as I did, that to feel love requires the right circumstances, the right families, or the right lovers. Our culture teaches us that we have to *find* love, and that the right relationship is what is required to feel love. Then, when we no longer feel the love we initially felt, we conclude that something must be wrong with the relationship, or perhaps with ourselves. But an entirely different experience of a relationship is possible when you bring love *to* the relationship, when the Universe brings you someone with whom to share that love. In that possibility, no one feels pressure to deliver love, and we are free to feel what we feel.

The seer's explanation points out another crucial distinction that most people never make, and that is the distinction between thought and the reality you perceive. Thought, and our perceived reality, live in two completely different domains. You can focus your attention on one or the other, but not both at the same moment. When you let the internal dialog die down, you focus on the perceived reality—the "world"—and you can then know what that world really is and who you really are, and that knowing is devoid of language. You are then free to experience the world as it is, without the intervening interpretation, without all the layers of meaning we have put on our experiences. In the world, the reality you perceive, there is no meaning. The so-called real world is just energy that has been stabilized or fixed in place and time by attention. And energy has no meaning; it just is.

All the meaning you believe you find in reality, in your actions, in who you think you are, is actually a function of thought. In thought, there is meaning. Again, the seer's explanation says that if you really pay attention to the distinction between the mind and the world, you will find that you can't think and experience at the same time. Because you can't focus your attention on both domains, thought and experience, at once, whenever you are entertaining thought you are dealing with memory, because what was perceived to be real is no longer present for you. That's what don Juan meant when he said, "We are perennially recollecting the instant that has just happened, just passed. We recollect, recollect, recollect."

Finally, every thought has feeling associated with it. When you entertain a thought, there is a feeling associated with thinking that thought, even if the emotional content is so slight you don't notice it. When we have ascribed sufficient meaning to a thought, however, we feel a strong feeling that is commensurate with the "goodness" or "badness" of the thought (i.e., whether it is an appealing or unappealing thought). Let's be clear about this use of "good" and "bad." In the seer's explanation, that distinction is not moral; morality lives in the domain of thought. Instead, the distinction lives in the realm of feeling, and every person knows when thoughts feel good or bad, though we typically collapse that distinction and say that it's *we* who feel good or bad.

The last distinction of the seer's explanation is that bad-feeling thoughts are rooted in the conventional explanation and its inclusion of the ideas of limitation, scarcity, inevitability, and so on. And good-feeling thoughts are rooted in pure beingness, in who we really are. These are the breadcrumbs with which we can find our way back, to who we really are, to the Garden.

A DIFFERENT CREATION MYTH

In this book I have described the manner in which we human beings have mistaken the description of the world for the world itself. My dear friend, Jan Diepersloot, offered in a letter an interesting restatement of this idea, which may further illuminate this distinction. I would like to quote it here:

I completely agree with the central thesis of your book: that the pre-requisite for genuine, transformative human experience is the ability to turn off our inner verbal spigot and stop our internal dialogue, or should I say, monologue. Only then can we begin to learn to relax, stop mistaking the map for the territory and re-learn to live in the world of concrete, felt experience as opposed to abstract description of experience.

Finally, I'm sure you will chuckle with me over the delicious irony of the fact that having travelled the territory, each of us, in our books, has drawn just such a map. In the final analysis, if we hope to point others in the right direction, we are forced to fall back on and use the very medium of words and writing to convey the dangers and pitfalls of mistaking them for the world they describe and map.

According to the seer's explanation, the fundamental building blocks of the world we experience are thoughts and feelings, not "fundamental particles" or space and time. We are each a unique cluster of feelings. Said another way, as individuals we are each a unique collection of vibratory modes of all-that-is, unique perspectives on the world that the Universe, all-that-is, has created. All of creation comes from nothing, the nothing that is also everything because in nothing is the possibility, the room or space, to create whatever can be imagined.

I started this narrative with the words, "...the first proposition to explore is whether we have a creation myth, and if so, what it might be." I say now that, viewed from the perspective of the seer's explanation, wherein what we mistake for the world is instead a description of the world, all that business about big bangs and the origin of consciousness is simply a creation myth. We weren't created; we have always been and will always be. And we create our world through interpretation and sustain it breath by breath.

Perhaps a story will help convey this better, so herewith I offer my own version of an arguably more appropriate creation myth...

The SUPREME BEING was sitting around one day, noticing that she was bored. She had created this beautiful world, with oceans, mountains, rivers, and creatures aplenty. All was in balance, light and warmth were provided, and well-being abounded. These were things she had thought of, and because the thoughts she'd had felt good, as did all the thoughts she thought, she thought them more, gave them more energy, and imagined their becoming reality. And that's what happened—they became real; after all, she is the SUPREME BEING.

The world ran perfectly. Creatures evolved and developed new attributes, because that's the way she imagined it, and that imagining felt good. Birth and death were a part of this joyfully balanced world, of course, because bodies wore out, and other ones needed to eat. And bodies were just temporary concentrations of energy anyway, and when death happened, the energy just freed itself and was available again for new forms of being.

But after a while, she was bored! While everything constantly changed, with the seasons, new creatures and all, everything also stayed the same. For a SUPREME BEING, you see, everything is good, everything feels good, and there's no meaning to any of it. When she noticed this boredom and recognized it for what it was, she suddenly had a new idea. She would have children! She would replicate herself (without the Supreme part, of course), and she'd have somebody to talk to and play with!

After a while, she wasn't bored any more, but the world she'd created needed something new. Since it was all perfect, she had no preferences. To create something new, you have to know what to change. So she gathered her children around her and said, "Hey kids, I have an idea!" Well, the kids knew what that meant…because her ideas always became reality. "Here's my idea: How would you like to go play in that world I created? You could have bodies, just like the animals, only different! You could play, you could dance, and you could be me in those bodies, with the ability to imagine and bring those imaginings into fruition!"

Well, the kids were excited, and they couldn't wait to get started. But then she said, "Hold on, I have to tell you a few things. First, you'll have to grow a body, just like the animals do. And to get started, rather than 'reinvent the wheel,' I'll start with some bodies I think will work just fine with a few tweaks. In fact, you can already see them evolving into something you will enjoy being in. Now, when you're born, you'll be in infant bodies that will require constant care for quite a while. In order to be me in physical form, you'll need sophisticated bodies, and those will take a while to grow.

"And here's the main kicker. Pretty quickly you're going to forget who you are and where you came from. You'll have to learn about the world from your parents, and other relatives, and teachers, and everybody with whom you come in contact during your early lives. That way you'll all be different, with different characteristics and different experiences, so that you can play off one another and learn from one another, and your imaginings and creations will be that much richer and more varied and interesting. Now these older and bigger people you learn from also will have been raised without memory of who they really are, and they may have not yet remembered that they can live freely, without lack and without worry, and so you may think thoughts that limit your ability to imagine and create. But each of you will have within you a lifeline back to me. And that lifeline will be that I, who am who you really are, my children, will always be present with you in your awareness.

"Sitting with me here, now, you have only ever felt love and appreciation for who you are. But when you're in the world, and when you haven't yet remembered who you are, you will feel other things, things that don't always feel good, because your elders, not knowing any better, will have taught you to think about yourselves and the world in limited ways that aren't consistent with who you really are. When things aren't to your liking, you will think you have to change them with your bodies, with action. Being my children, and thus in actuality being able to create effortlessly, you will discover that action is a hard way to change things. But within you always will be who you really are, because how could you not ultimately be who you really are? So to guide you back to who you really are, I will give you one desire, and that will be the desire to feel good. At some point, you will discover that some thoughts feel bad and others feel good, and you will want to feel good, so you will more and more think those good-feeling thoughts. And if you practice doing that, you will more and more be me, with full awareness of who you are and your ability to create according to your hearts' desires.

"Now don't forget that when you're done in the world, you will always come back here to be with me and be who you really are, pure energy. So you can't lose. Even if you insist on thinking thoughts that feel really bad, and in so doing attract to yourselves experiences that you really, really don't like, and you can't find your way back to who you are in your bodies because you can't find those thoughts that feel good, you will still come back to me and be complete again."

And with that, she created human beings to go forth into the world and expand the possibilities of being in the world. And inside each one is the possibility of remembering fully who they are and acting in the world for the sheer joy of it. The world is perfect, a composite reflection of all the thoughts that are being thought, ready to change into more and more beautiful forms as those children think better-feeling thoughts. As they remember who they are, they will see that nothing needs to be fixed because nothing is broken, and action isn't required to bring new possibilities into being. All that's required is to imagine, to want it to happen, and then to get out of the way.

THE END

Actually, it's just the beginning. I am always available (and eager) to work with individuals and small groups to further this conversation. I live in Carbondale, Colorado. I can be reached at: www.TheSeersExplanation.com

BIBLIOGRAPHY

Calbi, Evan. *Eudice Shapiro: A Life in Music*. Los Angeles: USC Thornton School of Music, 2006.

Castaneda, Carlos. *Tales of Power*. New York: Simon & Schuster, 1974.

Greene, Brian. *The Hidden Reality*. New York: Alfred A. Knopf, 2011.

Isaacson, Walter. *Einstein: His Life and Universe*. New York: Simon & Schuster, 2007.

Johnson, Simon, and Kwak, James. *13 Bankers*. New York: Pantheon Books, 2010.

Kemmis, Daniel. *Community and the Politics of Place.* Norman, Oklahoma: University of Oklahoma Press, 1990.

Puech, Henri-Charles. *La Gnose et le temps*. Zurich: Eranos-Jahrbuch, 1951.

Rosenblum, Bruce, and Kuttner, Fred. *Quantum Enigma*. New York: Oxford University Press, 2011.

ACKNOWLEDGMENTS

In addition to those teachers to whom I referred in my introduction, Carlos Castaneda (who is no longer with us in physical form), Werner Erhard, and Esther Hicks (who are), I want to thank several friends whose input has been indispensible in this effort. People who read the manuscript and offered valuable suggestions include Aleta Randall, Jan Garrett, Lisa Case, Amy Darosa, Pete Luboff, Michael Kennedy, Fred Kuttner (thanks for Figure 2!), Michael Rosenblum, and Jan Diepersloot. Others with whom I discussed these ideas to my great benefit include Luke Gottlieb, Kay Hagman, Barry Schwartz, Karen Wells, Barbara Wolf, Roxie Peterson, Bobby Mason, and JD Martin. The cover photo is courtesy of Luke Gottlieb. My "head shot" is by Bob Carmichael. Thanks to Vic Garrett for his memories of Liberty. Thanks to Nelson and Julie at Dos Gringos in Carbondale for a superb writing environment! And for just being there for me, Christine Falter and Kathie Engstrom, and of course, Mom and Dad.

Larry Gottlieb lives in Carbondale, Colorado. He can be reached at www.TheSeersExplanation.com.